On Christian Priesthood

On Christian Priesthood

ROBIN WARD

continuum

Published by the Continuum International Publishing Group

The Tower Building	80 Maiden Lane
11 York Road	Suite 704
London	New York
SE1 7NX	NY 10038

www.continuumbooks.com

Copyright © Robin Ward, 2011

First published 2011

British Library Cataloguing-in-Publication Data
A catalogue record for this book is available from the British Library.

ISBN: 978-0-8264-9908-0

Typeset by Fakenham Photosetting Limited, Fakenham, Norfolk
Printed and bound in India

Contents

Acknowledgements   vi

Introduction   1

1   Religion   8
2   Mystery   30
3   Sacrifice   53
4   Priesthood   75
5   Rite   97
6   Cure   119

Conclusion   141

Bibliography   152

Index   157

Acknowledgements

This book was written during a period of sabbatical leave at the beginning of 2010 and I would like to thank the Chapter of Pusey House, Oxford for providing such a congenial and erudite environment in which to pursue the task of writing. I am grateful also to my colleagues at St Stephen's House for enabling me to leave the management of the college in their capable hands for a term.

This book has exacted a toll of patience from my publisher, Robin Baird-Smith at Continuum, and I am thankful to him for his forbearance and encouragement. My family has been wonderfully tolerant of the expenditure of time and nervous energy which this book has demanded and for which they have lovingly borne the burden – I am hugely grateful to them for it all.

This book is dedicated to all the priests who have trained at St Stephen's House: *Devotedness of life is more important than solidity of labour* (Bishop Edward King).

Introduction

This book is a study of some theological themes which it argues are central to a proper understanding of ministerial priesthood in the Christian religion, but which have come to be seen as either unfashionable or redundant because of contemporary assumptions about what that ministry should be. In this sense it has an ambition to return to the sources: anxieties about ministerial identity in the contemporary setting have occluded fundamental aspects of sacramental theology, and in doing so have contributed to the loss of a proper conception of Christianity as a religion. When this happens, it becomes difficult to give any coherent account of what ministerial priesthood is and how it might differ from the priesthood which is common to all the baptised, either in character or in function. However, it is not a book which proposes a restorationist solution in which re-clericalisation restores morale and control to the priesthood as a class, nor is it simply an endorsement of the so-called 'hermeneutic of continuity', in which the legacy of the Second Vatican Council is exclusively appropriated by those who would see its reforms as necessarily dependent doctrinally on all that preceded them in the magisterial tradition of the Latin Church. I have great sympathy with this mood in contemporary Roman Catholic theology, not least in its liturgical sensibility, but in arguing for renewed attention to the theological significance of ministerial priesthood, I have found helpful and engaging allies among Anglicans like Richard Hooker, Orthodox like

Christos Yannaras and progressive Roman Catholics like Bernard Häring.

It is also a book which is interested in liturgy, but it is not a work of liturgical theology either. It is a truism to say that the twentieth century was a period of extraordinary liturgical innovation for Western Christians: both the transformation in the experience of going to Church and the historical resources newly available to those with an enthusiasm for liturgical revision have been prodigious. However, I think that liturgical theologians are sometimes rather less aware than they might be that the changes in practice they envisage coming about through alterations to texts and to buildings sometimes actually happen because of transformations in theological sensibility which are only remotely connected to their reforming agenda. Archbishop Cranmer wanted to restore more frequent communion in the Church of England, but despite his unique opportunity to re-shape the liturgical texts of the nation for the next four hundred years failed to do so. The sacramental practice which we take for granted today, in which all those in good standing (and indeed many who are not) participate sacramentally in the Eucharistic celebrations they attend as a matter of course, is not a consequence of earnest sixteenth-century exhortation, nor of the romantic revival which initially inspired the Liturgical Movement. It is a change of moral sensibility, perhaps the most radical transformation of lay piety since the age of Constantine, and it owes its success to the final eclipse of Jansenism in the moral theology of S. Alphonsus de Liguori, whose devotional temper is Neapolitan baroque at its most fervent, but whose re-working of moral theology made possible the participatory liturgical ethos of the present.

RELIGION

Attention to the moral character of Christianity is consequently fundamental to understanding how it subsists as a religion and how its expression in cult embodies the transformative grace which it promises and effects. Without this virtuous *cursus*, in which Christian living becomes the anticipation and incursion of beatitude into the life of the earthly city, there can be no liturgical integrity no matter how adeptly texts and rites might seek to supply its absence, and no ministerial priesthood that amounts to more than the sum of its various delegated functional attributes. Thomists of the strict observance have always been reluctant to call religion a virtue in itself, rather than simply a potential part of justice: for them it is something that is owed, albeit to God himself, and from this flows much of the positivistic functionalism of conservative Catholic sacramental thought in the West which is the curious *döppelganger* of much contemporary minimalism and suspicion of anything which might be branded as cultic. But there is another articulation of the role of religion in the taxonomy of Christian moral living, which proposes it as the co-ordinating principle of the theological virtues, orchestrating their efficacy in drawing the believer on towards beatitude and anticipating the vision of God by making the practice of the moral life cultic on earth as it is in heaven. This interpretation of religion as a virtue inspires Richard Hooker in his account of an ecclesiastical polity which intended to claim more than just functional justification for its visible ordering in rite and practice, and inspires Bernard Häring to construct a moral theology in which the active participation of the people of God is not simply expressed by how they might come to take part in religious services more actively, but by how they might live as orientated to adoration rather than obligation.

MYSTERY

If Christianity is a religion, then it is one which communicates grace and participation in the divine by sacramental signs. The sacramental principle is not unique to the Christian cult, and it is anticipated specifically in the rites and practices proper to the Israelite covenant. But the unique character of the Christian sacraments, their efficacy as morally transforming and participatory infusions of divine life in the particular circumstances of human living to which they properly relate, comes from the conformity of the Church to Christ as the originating and fundamental mystery, and the persistence of the mysteries of his incarnate life to eternity in the resurrection. The Christian cult is not simply evocative: it does not set out to inculcate an ethic of self-improvement through the activity of the community which offers worship in an edifying way, important though this might be. It is an enrolment, a true liturgy, in which the image of Christ is revealed in those who are called out by their participation, and incorporated into the eschatological communion of those whose worship orders their life towards their final end in God.

SACRIFICE

This is the case with each sacrament, ordered as they are to the various states and needs of Christian living, but it is true in an exemplary way of the Eucharist, which is a sacramental sacrifice and thus the exemplary work of Christ in the mystery of his high priesthood. For there to be a ministerial priesthood, there must be an authentic sacrifice for that priesthood to offer, and that sacrifice is consummated in the consecration of the Eucharist. Here I have been unsympathetic to the predominant understanding of this mystery in Anglo-Catholicism since the *Lux Mundi* theologians first gave some original attention to the notion of sacrifice in the Eucharist. The theology of the heavenly offering is obviously more appealing than the grim destruction theories which occupied the field in Latin theology from the sixteenth to the nineteenth centuries, and it has the added advantage of a good foothold in pre-Tractarian Anglican iconography. But for the sacrifice to be sacramental, it cannot but depend on the exposition of its meaning which the signs appointed give, not what may or may not take place invisibly as concomitant to the offering. Here I have found the clarity and precision of Dom Vonier's Thomist *ressourcement* my most reliable guide, not least because he also rescues the principle of Eucharistic concomitance from dreary controversy and employs it with such felicity to articulate the scope of what is sacrificial and what is not in the action of the Mass.

PRIESTHOOD

A religion which is sacramental and which has at its heart a sacrifice will have a priesthood to celebrate that sacrifice, and here I hope to encourage as authentic and sound a theology of ministerial priesthood which does not hesitate to express this ministry in terms of sacramental character. The priestly character of the people of God designates them as living a cultic life through their incorporation into Christ who alone is the definitive high priest by virtue of his obedience and atoning sacrifice. But this is not to exclude the ordination of a priestly character which is subsequent to Baptism and which subsists in the Church as a result of the Lord's commission to offer the sacramental sacrifice and the sacramental forgiveness of sins. In contemporary Anglicanism this understanding of character, which is present even in divines such as Hooker who deny the Eucharistic sacrifice, and which is quite clearly evidenced in the ecclesiastical law of England from the Restoration to the present, is now the object of some controversy. The association of Eucharistic presidency with presbyteral ordination is proposed as simply a matter of discipline, and ecumenical dialogue with the Orthodox has given an undue prominence to a particular strand of contemporary Eastern thinking which rejects the indelibility of orders (a prominence which perhaps reflects the internal controversies about canonical deposition among Anglicans in the United States). Neither understanding of the ordained presbyteral ministry does justice to the specific way in which the one ordained receives a character which delegates to cult, and so to a role of oversight in administering the sacraments which is not simply administrative but distinctive in its participation in the person of Christ who himself offers and himself endows with grace.

CULT

Although this is not a work of liturgical scholarship, the ethical character of the Christian cult as orientated towards beatitude necessarily means that the practice of that cult should reflect that fundamental character. Here I am most sympathetic to the contemporary emphasis on re-sacralisation and re-enchantment in the liturgy, because attentiveness to the setting and practice of worship is a fundamental part of the Anglican patrimony as articulated by Richard Hooker in the face of systematic iconoclasm and reductionism, and because the occlusion of glory as a concomitant of worship in the offering of the Eucharist inevitably comes to promote secondary pedagogic and pastoral considerations above the primary role of the rite, which is to offer worship which is perfect because it is Christ's. Again, the perennial Anglican sympathy with the platonic in theology complements the Augustinian emphasis on beauty as a transcendent in the liturgical writings of Pope Benedict XVI, and the Anglican experience of ritual revival in the most unpromising of legal and doctrinal settings gives confidence that even if a crisis of liturgical sensibility as grave as that outlined by the theologians of the Radical Orthodoxy school has taken place, it need not be irrevocable.

CURE

Lastly I turn to the cure of souls in its most obviously priestly manifestation, the sacramental forgiveness of sins. This is not intended to be a practical guide to hearing confessions for those engaged in pastoral ministry, nor an introduction to spiritual direction. But the forgiveness of sins in the practice of the Christian religion has both a ritual and a virtuous aspect: ritual because in attaching reconciliation with the Church to the forgiveness of sins as its outward sign, Christ makes the restoration of authentic liturgical enrolment constitutive of authentic ecclesial communion; virtuous, because uniquely in the sacramental dispensation a rite manifests a virtue, that of penitence, which is thereby taken up into the cultic orientation of the Christian moral life and definitively ordered towards beatitude. Penitence turns the Christian from sin by seeking amendment and forgiveness; by giving the virtue a sacramental character, that individual repentance is endowed with the sacral solidarity which the Church enjoys as the body of Christ. Historical factors have tended to obscure this in Anglicanism, where the devotional emphasis on the use of sacramental absolution has waxed and waned with the piety that produced it. By contrast, a renewed sense of what ecclesial re-enrolment might mean in an economy which does not seek to codify the moral life other than by the canon of martyrdom, as articulated by the Orthodox theologian Christos Yannaras, gives a more fruitful commentary on the medicinal character of the work of the ministerial priesthood in declaring the forgiveness of sins and restoring the broken bond of ecclesial life.

1

Religion

There are many religious people who are not saints, but all the saints are religious.[1]

Thomas Cardinal Cajetan

The premise of this book is that Christianity is a religion which offers sacrifice by means of a priesthood: the consequence of this is that the Christian moral life has a fundamentally cultic orientation. Attentiveness to the liturgical character of Christian living is not theological dilettantism, although much contemporary enthusiasm for the constant re-making of particular rites and ceremonies obscures this. To live liturgically as a Christian is to inhabit time and space in a way that anticipates beatitude; to live as a participant in the Christian cult is to fulfil what is owed to God in a way which orders the moral life as it is received by each Christian in Baptism. For Aristotle, virtuous political living in the city required above all for its right ordering the distributive force of justice to give each his due: without justice the other moral virtues can find no purchase in the commonwealth. The Christian moral life receives its orientation in the infusion of faith, hope and charity at Baptism, virtues called theological because they have God as their unmediated end. But these virtues need ordering in the life of the heavenly city just as the cardinal virtues require the presumption of justice in the earthly city, and it is the virtue of Religion which does this. Because Christianity has at its heart the sacramental offering of the sacrifice of Jesus Christ, and because the baptised people of God are designated in Scripture as the authentic priestly body in relation to the Father, so every moral act which tends to unite us to God is authentically sacrificial, authentically cultic in character. Augustine explains this when he says in *The City of God*: *True sacrifice is offered in every act which is designed to unite us to God in a holy fellowship, every act, that is, which is directed to that final Good which makes possible our true felicity.*[2]

The predominant ethos in the confection and presentation of liturgical worship in the Churches of the West since the 1960s has been demotic, synthetic, didactic and participatory. In particular the mode of celebration enjoined for the Eucharist has assumed that its fundamental character is that of a meal, and that the more this character is accentuated the better understood will be the complementary themes of sacrifice and offering.[3] But the introspective communitarian character of these celebrations has obscured with great harm the relation of cult to glory: without the apprehension of divine glory in the liturgy, what Lawrence Hemming has recently emphasised as the anagogical character of liturgical participation,[4] the moral vigour of the sacramental life loses its fundamental orientation towards beatitude, and dissipates itself in an essentially therapeutic manipulation of ritual acts for the sake of self-improvement. The repristination of the Christian cult as an explicit revelation of the divine glory is thus a moral imperative, not an aesthetic preference.

The Orthodox theologian Christos Yannaras expresses this liturgical, cultic character of Christian moral living in cosmological terms: *The ethos of the Church is liturgical not only because it unifies the people in the common work of the Eucharistic response, the response of thanksgiving to God's call and covenant, but also because it sums up the inner principle of the world, its meaning and end, in this Eucharistic relationship between creation and its creator. This is another*

9

way in which Christian ethics differ from any other philosophical, social or political ethics: they have a cosmological dimension, and do not make a distinction between the ethos of man's life, and the life and truth of the world.[5] The way in which liturgical worship sanctifies time and sanctifies place is therefore much more fundamental to the ethical tenor of Christian life ordered to beatitude and anticipating divine glory than any mere arrangement to assemble made for instruction, admonition and mutual encouragement, important though all these are. Liturgical worship offered by the ministerial priesthood appointed for this end and on behalf of the priestly people of God ought to elucidate the fundamental worth of the whole created order: humankind, called to participate in the divine nature and sanctified by the Eucharist for the promise of resurrection life; the inanimate creation, which from the time of the Tabernacle and the Jerusalem Temple has been represented in microcosm by the buildings and furnishings which house the divinely appointed cult, and which so enclose the act of sacrifice in a cosmological setting.

THE VIRTUE OF RELIGION

The climate in which the liturgical reform of the twentieth century took place has not been sympathetic to the inculcation of the virtue of religion, nor have the radical discontinuities in language, text and setting served to secure a stable liturgical identity in the lives of most Christians who have experienced these changes. Disaffection with the liturgical inheritance of the sixteenth century became most acute in the 1960s when the generation which had been young during the Second World War came to maturity. And it seemed that there was a strong case to be made against the traditional liturgical *praxis* of Western Christians: its legalism, its accentuation of controversial theological issues, its apparent incapacity to inspire anything other than derivative, 'ecclesiastical' arts, its failure to communicate Christian truth to the modern industrial worker or the under-catechised subject of despotic regimes, its ineffectiveness as a means of instilling moral courage in Christian peoples in the face of the totalitarian ideologies of the 1930s. However, the substitution for this inherited liturgical patrimony of synthetic rites which have to a considerable degree occluded the customary ordering of time and space in liturgical celebration by means of radical re-ordering, and the concurrent eclipse especially in Europe of the sort of social class structures much of the reform took as normative, have brought about a crisis of sensibility in liturgical culture which is now one of the principal anxieties of the pontificate of Benedict XVI. If there is to be a successful hermeneutic of continuity in response to this crisis, the ethical significance of the Christian cult must be fundamental to it.

RELIGION IN AQUINAS

The virtue of religion undertakes a critical but complex role in the moral taxonomy of S. Thomas Aquinas.[6] He inherits from Cicero[7] the classification of a number of virtues which are annexed to the cardinal one of justice because they have in common as their object something that is due, but which are termed potential rather than integral portions of justice because the rendering of what is owed cannot be reckoned by way of strict restitution. Religion is the first of these, and the most important. Religion pertains to Justice because it has as its object what is owed to God; but it is a potential rather than an integral part of that virtue because humankind can never satisfy its indebtedness to God, and so the obligation is always observed by way of what S. Thomas calls *excessus poenitentiae*. This is a striving which abandons any attempt to measure what is owed by resort to a reasonable mean, and which instead expends itself in the expectation of finding a merciful acceptance. Although Thomas is emphatic that religion in itself is not a theological virtue because it has as its end not

11

God but rather our acts of worship towards Him,[8] subsequent commentators in the Thomist tradition have been unwilling in their own analysis to treat the virtue as simply an aspect of justice, and have related it more closely to the operation of faith, hope and charity in the life of the Christian.[9] Indeed, when Thomas poses the question himself as to whether religion is in fact a theological virtue, he gives as authority Augustine himself for this view, who says *God is worshipped by faith, hope and charity*, even though his own conclusion is different.[10]

The pre-eminent excellence of religion as a moral virtue in the Thomist scheme has its foundation in the first three precepts of the Decalogue, which place what is owed to God by way of worship first in the moral ordering of human life. Moreover, according to Thomas, religion manifests itself in two kinds of act: those which it elicits which are proper to it, such as adoration and sacrifice; and those which it commands and so directs towards the worship of God, even though they are actually elicited by another virtue, hence the definition given in James of religion as care for the fatherless and widows (Jas 1.27). George Herbert expresses this distinction more economically when he says *Who sweeps a room, as for thy laws / Makes that and th'action fine.*[11] This power of religion to command other virtuous acts in the moral life and orient them towards God is of fundamental significance, and explains why many of those who followed Thomas Aquinas preferred to treat religion with the theological virtues even if they respected his argument against placing it among them formally. For the virtuous pagan, it is justice which oversees the reasonable mean in the exercise of moral living; for the Christian, infused with the virtues necessary for salvation at Baptism, every exercise of moral goodness is given a cultic orientation by the commanding power of religion. Every act undertaken with the intention of uniting us more closely to God as our final end attains through the directing power of religion the character of a true sacrifice: ethical living becomes liturgical living in the dispensation of grace.

Thomas is clear that the fundamental operation of the virtue of religion is internal: *We pay God honour and reverence, not for his sake ... but for our own sake, because by the very fact that we revere and honour God, our mind is subjected to Him; wherein its perfection consists, since a thing is perfected by being subjected to its superior.*[12] These acts he characterises as adoration, prayer and devotion: adoration, which is that reverence due to God because of his excellence; prayer, which is the devout elevation of the mind to God; and devotion, which is the will to give oneself promptly to those things that pertain to the service of God. However, he immediately counterpoints this with an affirmation of the sacramental character of those material signs which are necessary if we are to be aroused to spiritual acts: *Now the human mind, in order to be united to God, needs to be guided by the sensible world.*[13] So the act of adoration is one which has an internal aspect, the devotion of the mind, and an external aspect, which consists of the exterior humbling of the body. Here Thomas follows S. John of Damascus in expressing the common mind of both lungs of the universal Church: *since we are composed of a two-fold nature, intellectual and sensible, we offer God a two-fold adoration.*[14] The interior devotion of the mind is the first and most important part of the act of adoration but not its entirety: the bodily signs which are the mark of exterior adoration require by their character a consecrated place in which to take place, not out of necessity because God is in some way confined there, but because of the propriety which attaches to these acts.

S. Thomas describes the way in which adoration offered in a consecrated place is required for the sake of propriety in three ways: first, the incentive given to devotion by such a place, and here Thomas particularly mentions the Jerusalem Temple and Solomon's prayer in support of his argument; second, the holiness of the rites which churches contain and house; and third, the encouragement offered to those who pray by gathering with others to do so.[15] The consequence of this is that the built environment in which worship is offered and the respect given to its sacral character is integral to evoking the right ethical stance towards worship, the stance which is most conducive to eliciting the virtue of religion in all its acts. Lawrence Hemming makes this point pertinently when he says that the liturgical texts once prescribed for the celebration of a church's dedication exemplify the way in which its consecrated character evokes by way of a sign the divine presence which is shown but not confined by the signification: *O God, who invisibly holds together all things, and yet for the salvation of the human race shows the sign of your power, by your inhabitation of this temple make visible you power.*[16] Thomas gives as an example of this the importance of orientation in Christian public prayer: to face East for prayer corresponds to the movement of the heavens in revealing light; recalls the location of Paradise and thus our end in beatitude; and is christological because of Christ's identification with the East in Zechariah's prophecy.[17] It is not without significance here that the external form of prayer is linked not only to the ordering of space but also to the ordering of time, corresponding to the prophecy of Malachi about the perfect sacrifice to come.

RELIGION IN RICHARD HOOKER

The foundational Anglican divine Richard Hooker preserved the Thomist analysis of the moral law for the patrimony of the Church of England, and in so doing placed religion and the governing role which pertained to it at the heart of the well-ordered Christian commonwealth. Indeed, he declares that *pure and unstained religion ought to be the highest of all cares appertaining to the public regiment.*[18] Nor is this simply the enforcement of an outward conformity of rite and practice which curtails controversy and makes for peace: Hooker is clear that the proper practice of the virtue of religion is morally crucial in assuring the state is secure and well-served. Not only does public godliness invoke divine protection, it similarly qualifies both those who govern and those who rule with the necessary qualities to do so. Quoting Philo, he argues *if the course of politic affairs cannot in any good sort go forward without fit instruments, and that which fitteth them be their virtues, let Polity acknowledge itself indebted to Religion; godliness being the chiefest top and wellspring of all virtues, even as God is of all good things.*[19] Hooker is unwilling to call the Christian presbyter a priest because of the sacrificial connotation of the term, a reluctance which subsequent Anglican divines in the Laudian period do not share.[20] However, he is happy to call the magistrate a priest, because he considers that religion and justice are so naturally complementary that no true justice exists except where it is seen as an explicit work of God: *justice is God's own work, and themselves his agents in this business, the sentence of right God's own verdict, and themselves his priests to deliver it.*[21]

Hooker's argument makes religion both the source of individual virtue and the guarantor of public well-being: *we have reason to think that all true virtues are to honour true religion as their parent, and all well-ordered commonweals to love her as their chiefest stay.* Posed against this are, on the one hand, the assertions of the atheists, both those who ridicule the articles of the Christian faith and those like Machiavelli who acknowledge the importance of religion for social purposes, but see no need for its propositions to be supported in actuality; and, on the other, the Puritans who object to anything not explicitly sanctioned in Scripture as inevitably superstitious. Against them Hooker argues that *There is an inward reasonable, and there is a solemn outward serviceable worship belonging unto God. Of the former kind are all manner virtuous duties that each man in reason and conscience to God oweth. Solemn and serviceable worship we name for distinction's sake, whatsoever belongeth to the Church or public society of God by way of external adoration.*[22] This external adoration is ordered by divine command in its essentials and by human authority in many of its accidental forms, it being the character and quality of these latter which makes the substance of his argument with the Puritans. But the fundamental principle which Hooker establishes and defends through what now appear to be the most rarefied arguments concerning the sign of the Cross in Baptism and the observance of Christmas is the intimate connection between the efficacy of the external practice of religion and the manner in which the internal acts of religion which they sustain inform and shape the virtuous life.

Hooker is clear that, given the significance of religion as a virtue, close attention must be paid to the outward manifestations of cult in Christian practice: *that which inwardly each man should be, the Church outwardly ought to testify ... Signs must resemble the things they signify.*[23] And this is related not simply to the importance of good order, and the benefit of collective public worship in engendering devotion virtuous living for the good of the city. Hooker explicitly invokes beatitude and the expectation of the vision of God as the formative principle behind what is encouraged and what excluded: *Yea then are the public duties of religion best ordered, when the militant Church doth resemble by sensible means ... that hidden dignity and glory wherewith the Church triumphant in heaven is beautified.*[24] The criteria which he establishes for discerning what these public duties might be *as concurring with celestial impressions in the minds of men*[25] are threefold: intrinsic reasonableness; the test of antiquity; and the prescription of authority, or what he calls rather more attractively, *hanging our judgement on the Church's sleeve.*[26] From these three criteria Hooker moves immediately to a justification for those practices enjoined by the reformed Church of England but rejected by the Puritan party, beginning significantly not with particular ceremonies or rites but with the legitimacy of dedicating and designating as holy buildings in which the Christian cult is to be offered, arguing with S. Thomas from the precedent of the Solomonic Temple.[27] Having established

the importance of the sacral landscape, one in which not only
the existence but also the internal ordering of church buildings
and their dedication with splendour to the honour of particular
saints is defended, Hooker expends his energy in justifying the
entire spatial, ceremonial and temporal structure whereby
the Church of England asserts her character as liturgical, and
therefore orientated towards beatitude by her cult.

Hooker's ideal of an ecclesiastical polity is one in which
the virtue of religion instantiates the anticipation of beatitude
through an attentive appreciation of effective signs: the consecration of sacred places and times, the alternation of feast and
fast, the reasonable and venerable rites and ceremonies which
due authority sanctions and regulates, each ensure that the
sensible means of the Church's cultic life evoke the now hidden
life of the Church triumphant and so inculcate well-ordered
virtue in the commonwealth. All the more remarkable for
living in an iconoclastic age, Hooker is particularly sensitive
to the conservative character of religious cult in propagating
moral quality in those who experience it – buildings, times
and practices – because when well-ordered they signify the
divine glory to humankind, and require reverence, attention
and respect. Hooker's argument is far more than an appeal to
allow legitimate authority the right to settle matters of Church
polity which appear either indifferent or uncertainly founded
on Scripture; it is a moral argument founded in the virtue
of religion as the regulating principle of the godly state, in
which the end of humankind in beatitude is exemplified by the
provision of a devout public cult.

RELIGION IN BERNARD HÄRING

Hooker's vision of a Christian polity depends on the capacity
of the civil arm to achieve and preserve uniformity of use
throughout its territory, an ambition which by the end of the
seventeenth century was demonstrably frustrated, not least by

the reluctance of the English to accept his cultic conception of civic life. Nor since the unravelling of the European confessional states in the last two hundred years and the definitive recognition of the right of the individual to religious freedom by the Second Vatican Council is such a polity either feasible or desirable, perhaps most especially where it still manifests itself with a Cheshire-cat like insubstantiality in assumptions about the pastoral efficacy of the vestigial Church establishment in England. However, writing from a context formed by first-hand experience of the Nazi ideology and war on the Eastern Front, the moral theologian Bernard Häring returns to the virtue of Religion as a foundational element of his attempt to restore Christian ethics after the failure of the European societies in the first half of the twentieth century. Häring is clear that there is no possibility of reviving the confessional polity and that the experience of totalitarianism makes the moral responsibility of the individual a much more pressing contemporary priority in the ethical life than the preservation of the sort of Concordat Catholicism which attempted to delineate a privileged legal zone for the institutional Church in the Fascist state.

Instead, he takes as his starting point a distinction which originates with Rudolph Otto, between a sacral ethos and an ethos of sanction.[28] Within the ethos of sanction falls the common human area of temporal obligation, the content of which, if not its purpose and end, can be conceived apart from an appeal to religion. However, when religion informs it, the sanction imparted gives a foundation to the moral duties which are proposed and a vitality in carrying them out which stems from their new orientation towards the glory of God. There is therefore in this analysis space for the exercise of a common *phronesis* in the moral realm, in which Christians may and do act in co-operation with non-believers without necessarily assigning the modern secular polity to the realm of Augustine's organised banditry. This identification of the religious context as one which infuses moral activity with

a particular purpose and vitality otherwise lacking illustrates Häring's reluctance to accept the conventional Thomist
location of the virtue of religion as a potential part of justice:
it is contrary to the sense of sacred Scripture to look upon the
virtue of religion as a mere appendage and extension of human
justice.[29] He argues that although Aquinas was justified by *the
temporal kerygmatic reasons of his time* [30] in placing worship within
Justice, his treatment of the virtue in fact seems to contradict
this placement, in that *he gives to the whole moral realm the clearest
and sharpest religious orientation.*[31] Not only is religion the most
eminent of the moral virtues, it is also the one which is the
animating form of all the others, including those which are
strictly termed theological.[32] Moreover, he is emphatic that
the theological virtues of faith, hope and charity cannot simply
be excluded from *the visible experiences in this world of time and
space ... it is evident that the theological virtues reach out to meet the
virtue of religion establishing the foundation for its extension into time
and space.*[33] They are sacramental and communitarian as well
as personal, and as such the virtue of religion is indissolubly
united with them because unlike for Aristotle, the Christian
experiences the exercise of this virtue not as the payment of
a debt but within the context of the sacrificial Christ-event.
Häring concedes that the place of religion among the *cursus* of
the virtues is still open to theological discussion, but there is no
ambiguity about where his own sympathy lies.[34]

Because of this Häring is keen to develop the understanding
of religion given by S. Thomas as having the theological
virtues for its source and cause: *Religion is a certain protestation
of faith, hope, and love by which man is basically ordered to God.*[35]
He is moreover critical of the analysis which would place the
virtue of religion among the moral virtues simply because it
pre-supposes and requires a manifestation in space and time
in the form of cult, unlike the theological virtues properly so
called, which are ostensibly an unmediated dialogue with
God. In Häring's moral theology the theological virtues have

a profoundly sacramental structure which derives from the Incarnation and the sacrificial-cultic context in which the Christ-event frames the moral drama of Christian living. Even though unlike Hooker he certainly no longer sees the magistrate as the chief agent guaranteeing true religion, the sacramentality of his moral analysis can claim that *our entire activity in the world must have a religious formation, for all our acts must be ordered to the loving majesty of God. This means that all our moral tasks are at the same time religious tasks.*[36] Of a piece with this is his reluctance to accept that there might be an acquired, natural virtue of religious reverence which exists as it were prior to and alongside the infused virtue of religion.[37] For Häring, the authentic moral order is profoundly supernatural, insofar as it is entirely dependent for its force on its participation in the life of God.

What are the consequences of this analysis for Christian living? Häring is emphatic that to assert the primacy of religion as the organising virtue of morality should not in its turn eclipse those acts which are distinctive of the virtue properly so called, and which are in fact essential to its integrity. The sacramental character of the Christian life incorporates Christians into the high priestly ministry of Christ and constitutes a royal priesthood which possesses both objective sacral holiness and the anointing of the Holy Spirit to bring about an authentically interior deputation to cult. Moral rectitude is thereby consecrated to the divine glory, and as such does not have as its end an introspective self-perfection effected by ritual acts which are essentially meant as therapeutic, but a fundamental orientation to the glory of God. The key scriptural texts which Häring uses to support his exposition of the virtue of religion are drawn from first epistle of Peter[38]: the Christian is incorporated into a holy priesthood, and as such is commissioned to *offer spiritual sacrifices acceptable to God through Jesus Christ* (1 Pet.< 2.5).

CULT AND SACRED TIME

If religion is the organising virtue of the Christian moral life,
and therefore the theological virtues are infused in a moral
setting which is cultic and sacramental, the manner in which
this cult is offered is of fundamental importance, and emphatically not what Dean Inge suggested when he compared an
interest in liturgy to the collection of postage stamps. However,
external cult in itself is not enough: to be effective, the sacri-
ficial-sacramental environment must have a clear orientation
to beatitude, an eschatological expectation. Much of the most
recent critique of the liturgical reforms of the 1960s dwells
in particular on the way in which by making liturgical rites
simple, demotic and participatory they have been robbed of
this transcendent, eschatological character – they no longer
invite Christians to look to the East with expectation but at
the congregation of which they are a part. But the argument
is older and more fundamental than the particular development of the Liturgical Movement in the Western Church: it
emerges from the secularisation of the lived environment, the
contraction of sacred space. Catherine Pickstock has analysed
this contraction as a particular consequence of the privilege
given by the Enlightenment to mensuration: the reduction of
accurate knowledge to the fruits of measurement evacuates
liturgical living of its crucial eschatological aspect, the consequences of which are only too apparent in the mediocrities of
contemporary liturgical practice.[39]

Wagner's last opera *Parsifal* is a profound study of failed
cult which encapsulates Pickstock's argument exactly. When
Parsifal, the redeemer-fool, first stumbles across the Grail
community and is taken by the knight Guernemantz to see
the Grail ceremony, his new mentor tells him *Here time becomes
space*. And this is so: Titurel, the king's father, remains undead
in his tomb; Amfortas, the royal guardian of the Grail,
languishes with a wound that does not heal, caused by his sin

with Kundry who herself is held captive by her unchosen role as eternal seductress; the ritual is repeated but achieves no salvation for its participants. It is only when the innocence and courage of Parsifal break the enchantment that the priority of time over space is restored and the liturgical character of the Grail ritual as redemptive returns: the artificial and contrived beauty of Klingsor, the enchanter's garden, is overthrown, and in its place comes the seasonal blossoming of the Good Friday meadow. The Grail community has become dedicated to necrophiliac futility by its transformation of a cult in time to a cult in space; Parsifal, the Christ-like redeemer who brings healing through death, reinvigorates the liturgy by restoring its eschatology. Through their fall from grace the Grail knights have become unlikely Cartesians, and Wagner is attentive to the way in which this dissipates their cult of purpose or health. Once the right relation between time and space is restored, the liturgy of the Grail, far from being superseded by the events of the drama, comes to conclude them with a renewed splendour, now sanctioned by the direct intervention of heaven itself as the celestial dove descends on the Grail and Parsifal, its new guardian, while the other protagonists are at last released into death.

The observance of sacred time as well as the consecration of sacred place is thus an integral part of the orientation of the Christian cult towards its final end: the vision of God. Fundamental to this is the observance of Sunday, which as a corporate act of the virtue of religion on the part of the Christian community rests on an obligation which has its foundation partly in nature, partly in the command of the Decalogue and partly in the precept of the Church governing her external life. Around this fundamental observance of the Day of Resurrection as one of cult and rest revolves the whole seasonal and festal cycle of the Church's year, which is intended to mark the passage of time with a purposeful and revelatory sacred chronology. This revelatory character is clearly articulated by Richard Hooker when he says of those who observe a feast in honour of a particular Christian mystery by participating in the public cult and abstaining from ordinary work: *the very outward countenance of that we presently do representeth after a sort that also whereunto we tend, as festival rest doth that celestial state whereof the very heathens themselves which had not the means whereby to apprehend much did notwithstanding imagine that it needs must consist in rest.*[40] Although he does not exclude the educational and practical consequences of these observances, they are always placed in an eschatological context, acts of religion which anticipate our final end: *They are the splendour and outward dignity of our religion, forcible witnesses of ancient truth, provocations to the exercise of all piety, shadows of our endless felicity in heaven, on earth everlasting records and memorials, wherein they which cannot be drawn to hearken unto that which we teach, may only by looking upon that we do, in a manner read whatsoever we believe.*[41]

This characteristically Christian sanctification of time by festive public worship is always the target of hostility for those who wish to obscure the Christian doctrine of the glorification of redeemed humanity: puritans, whose theology of depravity will allow no idea of 'service' in the offering of worship; rationalists, whose utilitarian reduction of productivity to fabrication has no place for the ludic character of liturgical time; atheist revolutionaries, whose decimalisation of the week is an eradication from the face of time of the Sabbath rest. It is all the more unfortunate therefore that in our own time, having survived at some cost these assaults from outside, the Christian calendar is now most at risk from within. Liturgical revision has dislodged immutable times and dates from the popular memory and reduced much observance to a contrived bureaucratic mediocrity – Ordinary Time indeed. The reduction of festal days to the status of mere obligations to be discharged inevitably results in the absurd transfer of great feasts such as the Epiphany and the Ascension (not yet Christmas) to the nearest free Sunday, transfers which vary from region to region and which mortgage sacred time to the local ecclesi-astical bureaucracy. Even the commitment to the observance of Sunday wavers in the face of the relentless need to shore up attendance statistics: indifference to the perennial priority of the Day of Resurrection is simply re-branded as a 'Fresh Expression of Church'.

CULT ORIENTATED TOWARDS BEATITUDE

Attentiveness to what Hemming has called the anagogical quality of the external acts of the virtue of religion is of particular significance in relation to what Joseph Pieper in his analysis of Aquinas' ethical teaching calls purgatorial fortitude.[42] By this he means the courage that the Christian needs in order to enter eternal life. It is one of the fundamental superficialities of contemporary mission that the promise of salvation is preached as a self-evident good without any reflection on the moral bravery which is needed to inhabit a life in which the Christian will say: *It is no longer I who live, but it is Christ who lives in me* (Gal. 2.20). The astute mystic and doctor of the Church S. Teresa of Avila showed she understood this very well when she wrote: *I say that more courage is necessary to follow the path to perfection than to suffer a quick martyrdom.*[43] For this reason the saints are said to possess 'heroic' virtue, which is the courage to embrace in an exemplary and persevering way not only the resolve to die for the faith but also to enter willingly that purgatorial suffering which is the dark night of sense and spirit, to accept that *No man may see me and live* but to persevere nonetheless. To the Christian fortitude comes not simply as the natural virtue of bravery in the face of grave danger: it is a gift of the Holy Spirit, in which the soul receives confidence that it will attain eternal life, and so overcome not simply the danger which is immediate but each and every danger until it enjoys *utter freedom from toils and evils.*[44]

Now for the Christian to attain this courage, the practice of the expectation of beatitude must be a fundamental element of liturgical living, in which the microcosmic heaven of sacred place and sacred time houses rites that effectually signify the Petrine promise of participation in the divine nature. Orthodox commentators remind us of the experience recounted in the Primary Russian Chronicle which the emissaries of the Kievan prince Vladimir had when they attended the Divine Liturgy in the church of the Holy Wisdom in Constantinople: *When we went on to Greece, and the Greeks led us to the edifices where they worship their God, and we knew not whether we were in heaven or on earth. For on earth there is no such splendour or such beauty, and we are at a loss how to describe it. We know only that God dwells there among men, and their service is fairer than the ceremonies of other nations.*[45] But this capacity for inculcating the divine glory is not peculiar to the Eastern tradition; the anagogical quality of the Latin rite is a key theme in the liturgical revival of the nineteenth century, not least in the complementary hermeneutic of continuity represented by Anglican ritualism. Hemming analyses the classical Western understanding of sacramental causality codified at the Council of Trent in the phrase *ex opere operato* and parses it as a posing of the *eschaton* by every liturgical sign.[46] The gift of the Spirit in Baptism infuses the theological virtues, and thus makes possible the efficacy of the liturgical sign, not as made significant by the intention of the believer, but rather as effecting the recognition now in sacramental form of what will in the end be possessed by unmediated participation: *We hold by faith the ultimate purpose of the human to be the vision of God.*[47] But in order for this to take place, and so inculcate the fortitude requisite for dedicated Christian living with a fundamental orientation towards beatitude, the time, place and rite must have a sacred character, must be authentically and explicitly religious.

The virtue of religion in its ordering of the moral life as a sacramental reality and its designation of time and place and rite as sacred, articulates the biblical doctrine of the collective priesthood of all the baptised. In its external acts it serves to anticipate and to make present by effective signification the beatitude which is the true end of redeemed human living. As such it is inimically opposed to the utilitarian captivity of time and labour for fabrication and acquisition alone, and so fundamentally at odds with any equation of rest with time lost and dignity with extravagance. The Christian landscape of time and space is therefore a sacred one, inheriting from the transcendent mensuration of the Tabernacle and the Temple the ideal of its setting as a cultic microcosm of salvation history. The possibility of Christian moral living, given that it is only through the baptismal infusion of the theological virtues that such living can be, depends on the virtue of religion for its ordering and manifestation in the world just as the ethos of sanction depends on Justice: without religion the liturgical and sacramental character of ethical living is obscured and lost, and so with it the apprehension of divine glory which defines it. It follows therefore that the inculcation of this virtue by attentiveness to the character of the cult as an effective signifier of Christian truth about beatitude, and solicitude for the way in which the virtuous acts of religion secure this, is not simply an expression of aesthetic or antiquarian interest but a fundamental moral imperative of Christian living.

The controversies of the Reformation have narrowed the focus of Christian conceptions of sacrifice and priesthood in the West to very particular preoccupations with the way in which the Eucharist might be called the one and its celebrant the other. It will be the claim of this book that both these assertions are so, and that they follow from the cultic character of Christianity as such. But this sacrifice and this priesthood are not isolated portions of the Christian revelation, sustaining old controversies by a needless provocation. The ministerial priesthood and the sacramental sacrifice are proportionate elements of that more fundamental priestly delegation which commits the whole body of the baptised to a cultic life, one in which every moral act seeks to be religious and every religious act orders the life of grace towards salvation. Liturgical living is an ethical critique of any conception of time which is not eschatological, and any conception of space which is secular: as Lawrence Hemming has written, it is the liturgy which measures us.[48] It is also the school in which the people of God learn to exercise their priesthood, not by escaping from the exigencies of daily living into a sacred zone which anesthetises and insulates, but by reiterating the priority of the supernatural, and the truth which points to our end in the vision of God. S. Thomas Aquinas taught that to lack one virtue was to lack them all:[49] to lack religion is to lack the means to instantiate the gospel in the world – that is to say, the fundamental sacramentality which defines the Church and which makes her what she is, and what she is to be.

Notes for Chapter 1

1 Cajetan, Thomas, *In Secundam Secundae*, q 81 a 7.
2 Augustine, *City of God*, 10.6.
3 Typically, Lash, Nicholas, *Theology for Pilgrims*, p 203, 'Thus ... the straightforward answer to the question: 'What does the Mass look like?' is (or ought to be): a reading party followed by a shared meal.'
4 See especially Hemming, Laurence, *Worship as a Revelation. The Past, Present and Future of Catholic Liturgy*.
5 Yannaras, Christos, *The Freedom of Morality*, p 85.
6 Principally considered in Aquinas, Thomas, *Summa Theologia* II–II q 81 (hereafter *ST*).
7 *ST*, II–II q 80.
8 *ST*, II–II q 80.
9 The definitive eighteenth century moral theology of the Salamancan Carmelites considers religion immediately after the three theological virtues in its discussion of the first precept of the Decalogue: *Cursus Theologiae Moralis* V Tract. 21 Cap. 9.
10 *ST*, II–II q 80.
11 Herbert, George, *The Elixir* ll. pp 19–20.
12 *ST*, II–II q 81 a 7
13 *ST*, II–II q 81 a 7.
14 *ST*, II–II q 84 a 2.
15 *ST*, II–II q 84 a 3
16 Hemming, *Worship as a Revelation*, pp 7–8.
17 *ST*, II–II q 84 a 3.
18 Hooker, Richard, *Ecclesiastical Polity*, V 1 (2).
19 Hooker, *Ecclesiastical Polity*, V 1 (2).
20 Hooker, *Ecclesiastical Polity*, V 78 (2).
21 Hooker, *Ecclesiastical Polity*, V 1 (2).
22 Hooker, *Ecclesiastical Polity*, V 4 (3).
23 Hooker, *Ecclesiastical Polity*, V 6 (2).

24 Hooker, *Ecclesiastical Polity*, V 6 (2).
25 Hooker, *Ecclesiastical Polity*, V 6 (2).
26 Hooker, *Ecclesiastical Polity*, V 8 (3).
27 Hooker, *Ecclesiastical Polity*, V 11–17.
28 Häring, Bernard, *The Law of Christ*, vol II p 124.
29 Häring, *The Law of Christ*, vol III p 32.
30 Häring, Barnard, *This Time of Salvation*, p 157.
31 Häring, *The Law of Christ*, vol II p 125.
32 Häring, *This Time of Salvation*, pp 157–8.
33 Häring, *The Law of Christ*, vol II p. 122.
34 Häring, *This Time of Salvation*, p 157.
35 *ST*, II–II q 101 a 3.
36 Häring, *The Law of Christ*, vol II p 124.
37 Häring, *The Law of Christ*, vol II pp 125–6.
38 Häring, *The Law of Christ*, vol 2 p 128.
39 Pickstock, Catherine, *After Writing: On the Liturgical Consummation of Philosophy*, pp 46–100; 170–6.
40 Hooker, *Ecclesiastical Polity*, V 70 (4).
41 Hooker, *Ecclesiastical Polity*, V 71 (11).
42 Pieper, Joseph, *The Four Cardinal Virtues*, pp. 136–7.
43 Teresa of Avila, *The Book of her Life*, ch. 31.17.
44 Pieper, Joseph, op cit.
45 See Ware, Kallistos, *The Orthodox Church*, p 269.
46 Hemming, *Worship as a Revelation*, pp 80–1.
47 *ST*, Suppl q 92 a 1.
48 Hemming, *Worship as a Revelation*, p 158.
49 *ST*, I–II q 65.

Mystery

Those who want to look into the mysteries of Christ have in a sense to come out from themselves.[1]

S. Thomas Aquinas

THE MYSTERY OF CHRIST PERPETUATED
IN THE SACRAMENTAL CULT

S. Paul writes to the Corinthians that those who exercise the apostolic ministry should be thought of as *Christ's servants, stewards of the mysteries of God* (1 Cor. 4.1). The fundamental teaching of the New Testament about the mystery of Christ, expounded most fully in the third chapter of the letter to the Ephesians, uses the term to express the significance of the entire Christ-event: what was hidden according to the divine plan is now revealed according to God's wisdom in the fullness of time, a revelation for which the apostle has responsibility *to make everyone see what is the plan of the mystery hidden for ages in God who created all things* (Eph. 3.9). But the participation of the priestly people of God in this fundamental mystery is effectively realised through their fruitful offering of worship, and most particularly by their participation in the sacraments. The moral connection between the cultic sacramental life and the practice of Christian charity is made from the beginning: Ignatius of Antioch notes how the Docetists neither participate in the Eucharist nor show any attention for the afflicted or the needy[2]. So it is that the language of mystery which in the New Testament designates the manifestation of Christ in the world for its salvation becomes attached to the particular covenanted signs, by which redeemed human beings are incorporated into this mystery and enabled to inhabit a new realm of grace. This incorporation is no initiation in the sense implied by the pagan mystery cults, the content of which in any case is largely obscure. Christian sacramental participation always presumes a moral transformation in the individual, by which sin is remitted and life in Christ established and restored: S. Cyprian writing of his own Baptism says: *But as soon as the stain of my former life was wiped away by help of the birth-giving wave ... I was restored to a new manhood by a second nativity.*[3]

The nature of a sacrament as defined by S. Thomas Aquinas is *a sign of a holy thing, in as much as it makes human beings holy.*[4] Thomas follows Augustine in refusing to confine the sacramental economy to the Christian revelation, or even to those bound before it to the observance of the Mosaic law. He asserts that even if no particular rite was prescribed to human beings before the institution of circumcision which would serve as a remedy for original sin, such rites in the form of prayers and offerings made to God on behalf of infants are the common possession of humankind and so possess effectiveness as a natural means of testifying to faith. This he calls 'the sacrament of nature', and from it follows an understanding that pagan rites and ceremonies apart from the gospel can be seen as possessing some sacramental value, at least insofar as they inculcate faith and repentance.[5] This is not to derogate from the absolute primacy and efficacy of the sacraments of the New Covenant, which are established in the fundamental redemptive mystery of Christ himself; however, the persistence of the sacramental economy in the practice of natural religion anticipates the gospel and the fittingness of outward signs in accomplishing the work of redemption.

This sacramental principle applies not only to those outward observances which reflect natural piety, the instinct which leads the writer to the Hebrews to declare: *And without faith it is impossible to please God, for whoever would approach him must believe that he exists and that he rewards those who seek him* (Heb. 11.6). It is also present in a figurative sense in the rites and ceremonies of the Mosaic Law, which were effective insofar as they anticipated the work of Christ. The scholastic theologians wished to affirm the authentically sacramental character of the Mosaic dispensation while at the same time doing justice to the Pauline teaching about the inadequacy of the Law as a means of salvation. This they did by contrasting the operation of the sacraments of the New Covenant which fulfil their task *ex opere operato*, that is by effecting the grace which they signify, with the rites of the Law which have their efficacy *ex opere operantis*, by the act of those performing them as intended.[6] The only exception to this was considered to be circumcision, which was universally considered to remit original sin but not to confer the infusion of the theological virtues that only Baptism accomplishes.[7] The Pauline teaching on the inadequacy of the outward rites of the Mosaic Law to take away actual sin was reiterated in the Western tradition by both the Council of Florence and the Council of Trent, the latter of which summed up the common teaching by condemning the proposition: *If anyone says that those same sacraments of the new law are no different from the sacraments of the old law, except by reason of a difference in ceremonies and in external rites: Anathema sit.*[8]

However, close attention to the figurative quality of these rites demonstrates an anticipation of the Gospel which is significant for explaining the cultic delegation made to the *consecrated nation* of 2 Peter. In particular Margaret Barker has drawn attention to the way in which the ritual setting of the Temple and the rites which it contained anticipate and inform the liturgical tradition of the patristic Church at its most pristine and primitive.[9] Her exegesis of the role assigned to the

Bread of the Presence in the temple cult illustrates the specific
way in which the offering of the loaves and the character of
the cultic apparatus which accompanied this action anticipates a Eucharistic theme: the bread is not only holy in itself
but imparts holiness to those who eat it; the altar upon which
it is set has the same sacral character as the Ark itself; the
invocation over the bread makes it a vehicle for the divine
glory and the manifestation of the divine 'Face'; the 'spreading
out' out of the bread in offering makes it an anticipation of
the sacrifice of Christ himself 'spread out' upon the Cross.[10]
The scholastic tradition was willing to see in the priesthood
of Melchizedek an authentic sacramental ministry prior to
that of the Mosaic sacrifices. Barker amplifies this tradition
with particular attention to the theme of Wisdom, a feminine
aspect of the divine cult which is occluded by the Josian reform
of the Temple but preserved outside the reformed monotheism
of the Hebrew Bible to inform the liturgical meaning of the
Eucharist as sacrifice and participation. As Clement of Rome
writes, *Through Him the Lord permits us to taste the wisdom of
eternity.*[11]

SACRAMENTS AS SACRED SIGNS

How does the Biblical term 'mystery' come to be attached to
the particular sacramental rites which the Church celebrates,
and in particular to the Eucharist, which even the Book of
Common Prayer with its suspicion of anything evocative of
human offering persists in calling *holy mysteries*?[12] Crucial here
is the rendering of *mysterion* into Latin as *sacramentum*, a term
which had a transactional value in secular use which complements the sense of the sacred with one of solemn obligation.
It is in this sense that both Tertullian and Cyprian employ
sacramentum: for neither is it yet an exclusive technical term
confined to the description of particular significatory rites, as
both still use it to mean the mystery of the Christian faith more

generally.[13] It is the insight of Augustine which gives system and precision to sacramental theology properly so called, and attaches the concept of the *sacramentum* to those rites in which divine grace is conveyed by a sacred sign.[14] He did not insist on dominical institution nor necessarily on the unfailing efficacy of the sacraments, and so includes among their number some ritual usages such as blessed salt and penitential ash which the scholastic theologians excluded, although in the East this more expansive understanding remained uncontentious until the seventeenth century.[15] But against the Manichees he asserts the fundamental principle of the sacramental character of religious observance: *In no religion, whether true or false, can men be held in association, unless they are gathered together with a common share in some visible signs or sacraments; and the power of these sacraments is inexpressibly effective, and hence if contemned is accounted to be sacrilege.*[16]

Augustine's legacy to sacramental theology in the West is encapsulated in the phrase transmitted by Gratian and incorporated as a definition by both the Council of Trent and the Anglican Catechism of 1662: *Sacramentum est invisibilis gratiae visibilis forma.* This principle was developed by various medieval theologians who considered both the importance of dominical institution and the particular character of the Eucharist, in which the sign of bread and wine came to be understood as the same as the body and blood which they signified during the controversy with Berengar.[17] The fruit of this is summed up in the *Sententiae* of Peter Lombard, whose definition of a sacrament is the staple of medieval catechesis on this question: *a sacrament is precisely defined as such a sign of God's grace and such a form of invisible grace, as to bear its likeness and to exist as its cause.*[18] This definition fits exclusively those seven rites of Baptism, Confirmation, Penance, Marriage, the Eucharist, Holy Order and the Unction of the Sick which the Council of Trent defined as authentically sacramental, which classification the Reformers denied. However, despite this

movement towards precision and enumeration and so controversy, the principle of a sacrament as a mystery orientated
towards participation in the life of Christ as the fundamental
manifestation of divine grace was not eclipsed: both Hugh of
S. Victor and Pope Alexander III called the Incarnation the
first sacrament, after which Hugh places the Church as the
Body of Christ.[19]

MYSTERY AND PARTICIPATION

This sense of participation in the mysteries of Christ's incarnate
life re-emerges as a significant theological theme in the French
School of the seventeenth century, most particularly in the
writings of Cardinal Bérulle. He articulates this capacity for
redemptive participation in the 'states' of Christ's incarnate
life when he writes that the mysteries *are past with regard to
execution, but present with regard to their virtue, and their virtue will
never pass away, nor will the love ever pass away by which they were
accomplished. The spirit, then, the state, the virtue, the merit of the
mystery is ever present ... This obliges us to treat the things and mystery
of Jesus not as past and extinguished, but as living and present, and
even eternal, the source from which we can reap a fruit that is present
and eternal.*[20] The way in which this takes place in the soul is
at once both sacramental and virtuous. As S. Thomas writes:
*The humanity of Christ is the instrumental cause of justification which
cause is applied to us in a spiritual way through faith and in a bodily
way through the sacrament.*[21] It is this insight which finds liturgical
expression in the rite of Mass by the association of the phrase
Mysterium Fidei with the words and action of the consecration
in the Roman Canon: the virtue of faith is not the object of the
sacramental rite, to be edified and stimulated by the sign; it is
the Church's faith in the significance of the sacramental act
which recognises it as an intelligible sign, and so fundamentally consonant with the revelatory character of the mystery of
Christ. Augustine emphasises the importance of this ecclesial

faith in the authenticity of the sacramental sign as intelligible when he writes: *For take away the word and it is bread and wine; add the word and it becomes a sacrament.*[22]

This fundamental intelligibility of the sacraments, their congruence with the truth of divine revelation in the person and work of Jesus Christ, articulates their capacity to be not simply exemplary but also effective. John Henry Newman identified the Incarnation as *the mystery which established in the very idea of Christianity the sacramental principle as its characteristic.*[23] From this truth comes the capacity of the sacraments to effect what they symbolise, and so perpetuate the mystery of the Incarnation by participation and not simply by edification. John Saward points out that the extravagantly symbolic elaboration of liturgical rites which is characteristic of the ancient non-Roman liturgies of the West reflects a clear consciousness of the way in which Christ's humanity operates with a saving agency out of all his multifarious 'states' made present to us most especially in the Eucharist; he cites in particular the elaborate Eucharistic fraction in the Mozarabic rite, which recalls the principal mysteries of the Gospel as a preparation for communion.[24] Thus the fundamental mystery of Christ is as Bérulle writes *not past and extinguished but living and present, and even eternal, the source from which we can reap a fruit that is present and eternal.*[25] The sacramental economy is the objective means by which God causes this participation within the Christian; the mystery remains a mystery of faith because sacramental signification is set in an eschatological framework, only fully explicable in the light of the fundamental orientation towards beatitude which Baptism confers.

LITURGY AND SACRAMENTAL CAUSALITY

The connection between liturgical worship and participation in the mysteries of the redemption became a *locus* of theological controversy in the mid-twentieth century as a consequence of the work of Dom Odo Casel. Casel wished to emphasise that the mysteries of Christ were effective in an objective manner in the exercise of the Christian cult, and not simply subjectively by way of evocation. In doing so he gave considerable emphasis to the alleged parallels between Christianity and the Hellenistic mystery cults, and proportionally much less to the cult of the Old Testament, in doing so creating as Saward argues an unsatisfactory divorce between the historical figures of Jesus Christ and the *Kurios Christos* of the liturgy, whom he even named as a *Doppelgestalt*.[26] Subsequent official theology in the Roman Catholic Church has cautiously affirmed this objective presence of the mysteries in the cult without endorsing Casel's somewhat tentative and unsystematic account of it. Pius XII stated in *Mediator Dei*, the principal liturgical encyclical of his pontificate given in 1950, that these liturgical mysteries are *shining examples of Christian perfection, as well as sources of divine grace, due to the merit and prayer of Christ. They still influence us because each mystery brings its own special grace for our salvation.*[27] Although *Sacrosanctum Consilium*, the Constitution of the Second Vatican Council on the sacred liturgy, only states that the mysteries of the redemption are present to us now *in some way*,[28] the *Catechism of the Catholic Church* embraces the theology of the French school wholeheartedly in its exegesis of the mysteries, quoting as its authority S. John Eudes when it says: *For it is the plan of the Son of God to make us and the whole Church partake in his mysteries and to extend them to and continue them in us and in his whole Church.*[29]

Lawrence Hemming argues that an appropriate theology of liturgical mystery re-orientates the understanding of what worship achieves from a contemporary mistaken assumption that the assembly gathers to performs a liturgical action, to a model in which the work which Christ himself performs manifests the assembly as an authentic *ecclesia*.[30] The liturgy, specified as meaning the public service due from an individual, derives from an already made enrolment of the individual into a laity, which itself designates inscription into a sponsoring headship. So the Christian liturgy, far from being simply the gathering of the assembly to perform certain acts and practices which produce a work, is rather the effective recapitulation of the fundamental movement of mystery from concealment to disclosure: as the mystery of the Word in relation to the Father is hidden and then revealed in the Incarnation, so in the liturgy the same revelatory work of Christ is continued and made manifest in a way which definitively convokes the people of God by the visible sign of the *sacramentum*. This is why the virtue of religion works as the instantiated ground for the theological virtues in the cultic arena of Christian moral living, and why the fundamental priestly enrolment of the baptised in the new Covenant is made tangible by the perfect exercise of the virtue of religion which the divine Christ exercises on our part before the Father in the Incarnation and on the Cross.

Hemming's account of the priority of Christ's work in the sacramental dispensation makes him impatient of much of the scholastic analysis of sacramental causality in the Latin tradition. Five models of causality are apparent in the treatment of this issue by the scholastic theologians.[31] Occasional causality ascribes the efficacy of each sacramental administration to a decree of the divine will guaranteeing the gift of grace whenever the sacrament is duly administered, a view favoured in particular by the Nominalist school. Moral causality ascribes a moral worth to each sacrament in itself, which in turn causes God to grant grace to the recipient, which explanation, when the moral value is ascribed to Christ as principal minister and celebrant of each sacrament, comes near to the mystery-presence theory of Odo Casel. Perfective physical causality declares that the sacramental rite itself is an immediate physical cause of grace: perfective, because the rite itself causes the grace to be given without any symbolic inter-mediation; physical, because the effectiveness of the sacrament does not depend on its character as a sign, which is simply a complementary enhancement of its divine instrumentality. Dispositive physical causality proposes that the symbolic reality communicated to the recipient in the sacramental rite causes a disposition to grace which God fulfils with the concomitant gift of grace according to the usual working of his providence. Dispositive intentional causality agrees with this analysis in identifying the effectiveness of the sacrament with the manifestation of an appropriate disposition to receive grace, but for the physical account of how this grace is given substitutes an expression of the divine intention to sanctify, which when expressed is then actually produced.

Against these somewhat arid accounts of how grace is given in the sacramental order the Jesuit theologian Bernard Leeming argued for a Thomist position given originally in the *Commentary on the Sentences* and then subsequently obscured by the commitment of later scholastics to express the problem in terms of exclusively Aristotelian causality.[32] This relates efficacy to the symbolic reality of each sacrament, and in particular explains it by the way in which fruitful reception of the sacraments brings the requisite appropriate grace through the establishment of a special unity between the properly-disposed recipient and the Mystical Body of Christ. Such an understanding depends, as Leeming says, on recovering the fundamental sacramental insight that Christ is himself the mystery – the *sacramentum* – that precedes all others, both as the hidden truth of God now revealed and as the promise and guarantee of salvation for humankind to come. Consequently the Church herself as his Mystical Body is likewise a sacrament in being the sign and cause of salvation in the world, into the supernatural vitality of which the individual is grafted by participation in the symbolic realities of each specific sacramental rite. This incorporation is neither simply moral nor simply physical: it is supernatural and spiritual, because these are the characteristics of the Body into which sacramental enrolment takes place.

SACRAMENTAL CULT IN RICHARD HOOKER

Richard Hooker in his defence and exposition of the sacra-mental practice of the Church emphasises precisely this maternal character of adoption into a new creation which Baptism initiates and the Eucharist sustains: *The Church is to us that very mother of our new birth, in whose bowels we are all bred, at whose breasts we receive nourishment.*[33] He notes that for the Fathers *all duties of religion containing that which sense or natural reason cannot of itself discern, are most commonly named sacraments,*[34] but himself confines the usage more strictly to those ceremonies in which the substance is visible, but a *sacred and secret gift* given in their reception. Hooker is clear about the eschatological reference of sacramental worship: *Sacraments are the powerful instruments of God to eternal life.*[35] Hooker then expounds this point at some length by establishing the basis of sacramental eschatology in the personhood of the incarnate Christ, in particular by arguing that although Christ's humanity is by its nature local and not ubiquitous, yet because *his bodily substance hath every where a presence of true conjunction with the Deity* it therefore has by virtue of its dignity as the body of the Son of God, a *presence of force and efficacy throughout all the generations of men.*[36] This Hooker calls omnipresence by sacrificial virtue: the human nature made a sacrifice for sin has no ubiquity of itself, but is *infinite in possibility of application.*[37] From presence he moves to participation: *Participation is that mutual inward hold which Christ hath of us and we of him, in such sort that each possesseth other by way of special interest, property, and inherent copulation.*[38] This participation depends on the incorporation of the saints into the perfect love which the Father has for the Son and the perfect filial adoration which the Son offers as incarnate, and so is fundamentally a participation within the economy of the Mystical Body: *For his Church he knoweth and loveth, so that they which are in the Church are thereby known to be in him.*[39]

To say that this participation is simply a matter of having a common human nature Hooker calls *too cold an interpretation*

... *It is not this that can sustain the weight of such sentences as speak of the mystery of our coherence with Jesus Christ.*[40] Instead *the Church is in Christ as Eve was in Adam,* a spousal union which he affirms in terms of its sacrificial virtue when he explains: *The Church he frameth out of the very flesh, the very wounded and bleeding side of the Son of man.*[41] Hooker then distinguishes the presence of Christ in his Church which is *whole with every part of the Church, as touching his Person,* but distinct to the individual *as a true actual influence of grace whereby the life we live according to godliness is his.*[42] Hence our participation in Christ is partly by imputation of his merits and partly by *habitual and real infusion* of grace, both in this life and more fully in the life of the world to come.[43] Consequently the sacramental economy takes its foundation from this participatory premise: *They are heavenly ceremonies, which God hath sanctified and ordained to be administered in his Church, first, as marks whereby to know when God doth impart the vital or saving grace of Christ unto all that are capable thereof, and secondly as a means conditional which God requireth in them unto whom he imparteth grace.*[44]

When Hooker considers sacramental causality, he rejects the principle that they convey grace *ex opere operato,* but in so doing demonstrates that he associates this explanation with the strictly physicalist analysis of how each sacrament conveys grace.[45] He adopts instead the moral explanation of their efficacy: *That saving grace which Christ originally is or hath for the general good of his whole Church, by sacraments, he severally deriveth into every member thereof. Sacraments serve as the instruments of God to that end or purpose, moral instruments, the use whereof is in our hands, the effect in his.*[46] Similarly, he preserves the distinction between the specific graces bestowed by each sacrament (which he numbers as two): *Yet then doth Baptism challenge to itself but the inchoation of those graces, the consummation whereof dependeth on mysteries ensuing.*[47] Thus the character of the participation in Christ which the worthy recipient obtains in each sacrament has both a common element and a particular one: *the participation of Christ which properly belongeth to any one sacrament, is not*

41

otherwise to be obtained but by the sacrament whereunto it is proper.[48] The outward form of the sacrament is indicated as appropriate by the inward grace conveyed, in the same way in which the soul orders the naturally expedient substance and accidents of the body. Hooker expands this definition of outward form to include both the substance of the outward sign and the form which the elements receive from the declaration of the Dominically instituted sacramental words. Here the Augustinian argument from intelligibility is reaffirmed: *it was of necessity that words of express declaration taken from the very mouth of our Lord himself should be added unto visible elements, that the one might infallibly teach what the other do most assuredly bring to pass.*[49]

Hooker concludes his consideration of the sacraments in general with a definition of sacramental intention which significantly amends that of the first generation of Anglican reformers and returns to the scholastic position. Bishop Jewel had called the principle that the minister of the sacrament must intend to do what the Church does the *very dungeone of uncertainty*, given the disagreement between East and West which he perceived over transubstantiation and the form for consecrating the Eucharistic elements.[50] Hooker re-affirms the character of the sacraments as *actions religious and mystical*, which for their authenticity it is sufficient that *the known intent of the Church generally doth suffice, and that we may presume that he which outwardly doth the work, hath inwardly the purpose of the Church of God.*[51] This is in contrast to the Lutheran view that only the faith of the recipient was significant, and expresses an understanding of intention which is compatible with the teaching of the Council of Trent, albeit by holding it necessary to use the sacramental form seriously, rather than form a specific mental intention to act as the Church intends. Thus Hooker establishes the sacramental economy as the necessary concomitant of the virtue of religion following the Incarnation: sacramental rites are mystical and religious; have as their origin the sacrificial virtue of Christ's efficacious glorified humanity; and receive intelligible integrity from Him in the eschatological faith of the Church.

THE NATURE OF SACRAMENTAL GRACE

What is the character of the grace which the Christian receives in the sacraments? The multiplicity of the sacraments and their character as symbolic causes which contain the grace they signify proposes that the help given will be different depending on what is so signified. Sanctifying grace infuses the theological virtues, gives the will specific inclinations through the seven-fold gifts of the Holy Spirit, and gives a supernatural elevation to the natural virtues. Two different views pertain among the scholastic theologians as to how this sanctifying grace is given in the sacraments. The Scotist school asserts that the reception of the sacrament gives the recipient a title to actual graces which are needed to fulfil the purpose of the sacrament, but that the character of this grace is simply the same as sanctifying grace *per se*.[52] The other view, which has its foundation in S. Thomas Aquinas,[53] sees sacramental grace as distinct from sanctifying grace because it is an infused habit, and therefore akin to the vitality which membership of the Mystical Body of Christ conveys rather than the establishment of that life itself with incidental reinforcement. S. Thomas calls these perfections *a kind of emanation from the grace of which we are speaking, just as are the virtues*.[54] This vitality acknowledges the foundation of the sacramental economy in the order of redemption by being directed primarily towards healing and restoration: the disorder of human personality and character is re-conformed by sacramental participation so that the Pauline aspiration of living only with the life of Christ is realised with what Leeming calls the character-determinants of sacramental grace.

However, the sacramental economy is not confined to the effect which it produces in the sanctification of Christians: the celebration of the sacraments, and in particular the Eucharistic sacrifice, is in itself an act of worship directed to God. Anscar Vonier, the principal English-speaking theologian of the Eucharistic mystery in the twentieth century and indeed also the principal opponent of any sense of heavenly offering in the Eucharist, was still able to say that the Mass is *more truly a sacrament through the worship of God than through the sanctification of man.*[55] This cultic orientation of the sacramental economy depends on the action of the person of Christ in each sacrament with intention to sanctify, the power of this sanctification coming from the representation of the Passion which the Eucharist effects pre-eminently, and which is the fundamental priestly sacrifice of the Christian religion. The celebration of the sacraments is thus not confined in their efficacy to the grace given to us vicariously by Christ through rites in which a symbolic reality is given; sacramental worship is cultic because it is the liturgy of the Mystical Body of Christ, and thus definitively conformed to his own priestly work. Although it is in the Eucharist that this work of worship is primarily accomplished, nevertheless the other sacraments participate in this cultic character because of their representation of the Passion in their proper work. This S. Thomas Aquinas articulated when he defined sacramental grace as being for two ends: *to take away the defects consequent on past sins ... and further, to perfect the soul in things pertaining to Divine Worship in regard to the Christian Religion.*[56]

THE ESCHATOLOGICAL CONTEXT
OF SACRAMENTAL CULT

This temporal reference of the sacramental economy, which is at once both historical and eschatological, makes the moral significance of cultic participation for the Christian much more than a work of simple self-improvement. It is an initiation and incorporation into the entire Christ event and thus the entire history of salvation, so assimilating the Christian to the

44

glorified Lord who will return. This assimilation is both to his Passion and death, which therefore give our own suffering and death an eschatological value, and to his glory, by which we are endowed with the grace of deification in anticipation of beatitude. Bernard Häring argues that *sacramental piety and morality are essentially ordered to the Second Coming, for the Holy Spirit sent to us is the gift of the glorified and risen Christ, the grace infused into us is directed to the eternal glory of God to be manifested in the parousia*.[57] For Häring, the sacramental system as a whole testifies to the apocalyptic character of Christian living, in which the witness of the Christian is not only to *give painful testimony to the truth before Pilate and this world*,[58] but to anticipate the finality of divine glory and the certainty of redemption in the trauma of the ongoing struggle against sin and suffering. Because of this, the obligation to participate in the sacraments which the Church has imposed on her members from the beginning, and in particular the requirement to communicate at Easter, is not simply a canonical norm or piece of empty formalism; it is the conscious designation of each Christian life as subject to the objective value and meaning of Christ's work in history and his coming in glory at the end.

John Zizioulas emphasises this eschatological character of sacramental participation in his own consideration of the Eucharist. The Eucharist in its two-fold character as visitation and tabernacle enables divine glory to be experienced as truth in communion.[59] This truth is neither exclusively propositional nor transmitted simply by historical contingencies; it is engendered out of the community because of its sacral character, and has a primarily soteriological purpose in revealing the true icon of Christ undistorted by error and sin. Zizioulas characterises this process as one of *acceptance, sanctification and transcendence*: a Eucharistic movement from the created order to glorification in communion which serves as the template for a process by which the elevation of dogmatic truth from the raw material of human history and culture to the Pentecostal imaging of Christ in the present takes place in the nexus of the Church.[60] This gives the Christian moral life a distinctive sacramental freedom: freedom in communion is no longer freedom to choose in a fallen condition between good and evil; instead it becomes a freedom which in the light of the Christ-truth about creation no longer proposes a choice which divides, but rather one that answers an unambiguous *yes* to the truth of the Gospel in the Eucharistic *Amen*.[61] Individualisation is transcended by communion, and so moral freedom is advanced into ontological freedom. This finds its expression through the truth of Being in Communion: the alleged finality of death is denied by the promise of glory anticipated in the Eucharistic action.[62]

THE CHURCH AS SACRAMENT

The sacramental character of the Church, present in the treatment of the sacramental economy by some of the scholastic theologians but subsequently obscured by the positivist character of most Counter-Reformation manualist dogmatics, re-emerges with some vigour in the teaching of the Second Vatican Council. The dogmatic Constitution on the Church *Lumen Gentium* deliberately restores the character of the Church as a Mystery of Christ, which Pope Paul VI elucidated by calling her *a reality imbued with the hidden presence of God*.[63] The Constitution introduces the theme of sacramentality immediately by referring to the Church as *in Christ as a sacrament or instrumental sign of intimate union with God and of the unity of all humanity*.[64] This is complemented and enforced by the exegesis of the Church's reality in terms of biblical images rather than scholastic terminology: the priority of the symbolic here articulates the character of the mystery as both hidden and authentic. The Constitution declares that *the sacred character and organic structure of the priestly community* is brought into being through *the sacraments and the exercise of the virtues*.[65] This intimate connection between cult and morality is emphasised by the definition of Baptism which follows, in which the faithful are by the baptismal character given a place in the worship of the Christian religion (*ad cultum religionis christianae charactere deputantur*).[66] This consecration is particularly exemplified in the Eucharist, *the source and culmination of the whole Christian life*, in which the priestly people *offer to God the divine victim, and themselves along with him*.[67]

The orientation of the mystery of the Church towards beatitude is examined in the seventh chapter of the Constitution: the Church *will reach its completion only in the glory of heaven*, even while in the course of history she acts as *the universal sacrament of salvation* through whom Christ makes human beings *sharers in his glorious life* through participation in his own body and blood.[68] This eschatological context of the Church's presence in time was seen by some commentators as a move from an essentialist to an existentialist self-understanding: Christopher Butler called it *an affirmation of the historical and metachronic against the essentialist, ultimately philosophic or metaphysical, view of the Church*.[69] However, the Constitution in fact goes on to express its understanding of the eschatological character of the Church in terms of sacrament and cult: our common bond with the saints in heaven is the sacred liturgy, when by offering the Eucharistic sacrifice *we join very closely the worship of the heavenly Church*.[70] Recapitulation of salvation history, the communication of the mysteries of grace which that history secures, and the cultic anticipation of the vision of God in communion with the saints who now enjoy it, gives to the Church its fundamental character of universal sacrament, from which prior reality its hierarchical and jurisdictional structure derives. The significance of *Lumen Gentium* in this respect is to re-emphasise dogmatically the orientation of the sacramental economy towards beatitude, and thus its intelligibility in the light of the eschatological hope of the Church.

SACRAMENTAL WORSHIP AND
THE MYSTERY OF CHRIST

If the virtue of religion articulates the cultic character of the Christian moral life in its orientation towards beatitude, then the sacramental economy is the means whereby the mystery of Christ who is both archetypal priest and archetypal sacrament becomes the vital infusion of the life of grace in the designated priestly people of the new covenant. Sacramental worship has its anticipation in the external rites of natural religion, and a more specific symbolic designation in the ritual practices and setting of the Mosaic Law and Solomonic cult. These derive their efficacy not from themselves but from the way in which as cultic anticipations of Christ they dispose their participants to faith and repentance. Jesus Christ in his incarnation definitely institutes the sacramental order of salvation through the symbolic revelation of his eternal divinity through the medium of his authentic humanity: this fundamental Mystery is so characterised because it is both the manifestation of what was hidden according to God's purpose, and a covenant which establishes the eschatological hope of beatitude definitively within the temporal sphere. The mysteries of Christ's incarnate life are communicable through the sacraments by virtue of the persistence of these mysteries to eternity in the order of salvation. These mysteries inform the accommodation of sacramental grace to the need of fallen humanity by the symbolic specification of each sacramental rite to the particular states of the people of God as delegated to cult.

The character of the Church as universal sacrament derives exclusively from her spousal character as Christ's Body, and makes of liturgical worship not the work of an assembly undertaken to effect a particular ethic of self-improvement, but a manifestation of intelligible eschatological truth made by the One who is the fundamental sacrament and who in so doing designates and constitutes his own Body. The truthfulness of the Eucharist as the pre-eminent exercise of the Christian cult in revealing the authentic image of Christ depends on this capacity to imbue the temporal with an authentic orientation to beatitude, for it is the incursion of beatitude into the temporal order which makes the cult salvific. The sacraments heal and restore, for they are instituted for the benefit of a fallen race; but in doing so they designate and enrol a priesthood which is eternal because the high priesthood on which it depends is eternal. For this reason the celebration of the sacraments, and in particular the offering of the Eucharistic sacrifice, require for their symbolic integrity an appropriate reverence for and anticipation of divine glory as presence and promise. Without this sense of the numinous the eschatological context of the Christian cult risks being obscured by a celebration which becomes pragmatic and self-referential, thus obscuring what it is meant to manifest. With it, the Church in her sacramental life becomes the place of visitation and the tabernacle of the presence, the place where the divine glory constitutes the people of God and through the virtuous exercise of religion orders their moral life towards the eschatological realisation of Mystery at the Second Coming of the Lord.

Notes for Chapter 2

1 Aquinas, Thomas, *Expositio in evangelium Ioannis*, 20.
2 Ignatius of Antioch, *Letter to the Smyrnaeans*, 7.
3 Cyprian, *Ad Donatum*, 4.
4 *ST*, III q 60 a 2.
5 *ST Suppl*, q 61 a 3; q 70 a 4.
6 Council of Florence, *Decretum pro Arminiis*, in Tanner, Norman & Alberigo, Giuseppe, *Decrees of the Ecumenical Councils* vol 1 p 541.
7 *ST*, Suppl, q 70 a 4.
8 Council of Trent, Session 7, Canon 2 in Tanner & Alberigo, *Decrees*, vol 2 p 684.
9 See Barker, Margaret, *Temple Theology: An Introduction*.
10 Barker, Margaret, *Temple Theology: An Introduction* pp 84–6; *The Hidden Tradition of the Kingdom of God*, pp 125–6.
11 I *Clement* 36.
12 *The Book of Common Prayer*, Third Long Exhortation from the communion service.
13 Leeming, Bernard, *Principles of Sacramental Theology*, p 561.
14 Leeming, *Principles*, pp 561–2.
15 Leeming, *Principles*, p 563.
16 Augustine, *Answer to Faustus, a Manichaean*, 19, 11.
17 Leeming, *Principles*, pp 564–5.
18 Lombard, Peter *Sententiae*, 4, 7.
19 Leeming, *Principles*, pp 366–7.
20 Bérulle, Pierre de, *Opuscules de Piété*, p 241. Translations of Bérulle are given from Saward, John, *Cradle of Redeeming Love* (see note 24 in this chapter.)
21 Aquinas, *Questiones disputate de veritate*, q 27 a 4.
22 Leeming, *Principles of Sacramental Theology*, p 58.
23 Newman, John Henry, *An Essay on the Development of Christian Doctrine*, p 325.

24 Saward, John, *Cradle of Redeeming Love*, p 98.
25 Bérulle, Pierre de, *Opuscules de Piété*, p 241.
26 Saward, *Cradle of Redeeming Love*, p 67.
27 Pope Pius XII, *Mediator Dei*, 163–5.
28 *Sacrosanctum Consilium*, 102 in Tanner & Alberigo, *Decrees*, vol 2 p 838.
29 *Catechism of the Catholic Church*, p 521.
30 Hemming, *Worship as a Revelation*, pp 77–8.
31 Leeming, *Principles of Sacramental Theology*, pp 287–94.
32 Leeming, *Principles of Sacramental Theology*, pp 347–55.
33 Hooker, Richard, *Ecclesiastical Polity*, V 50 (1).
34 Hooker, *Ecclesiastical Polity*, V 50 (2).
35 Hooker, *Ecclesiastical Polity*, V 50 (3).
36 Hooker, *Ecclesiastical Polity*, V 55 (9).
37 Hooker, *Ecclesiastical Polity*, V 55 (9).
38 Hooker, *Ecclesiastical Polity*, V 56 (1).
39 Hooker, *Ecclesiastical Polity*, V 56 (7).
40 Hooker, *Ecclesiastical Polity*, V 56 (7).
41 Hooker, *Ecclesiastical Polity*, V 56 (7).
42 Hooker, *Ecclesiastical Polity*, V 56 (10).
43 Hooker, *Ecclesiastical Polity*, V 56 (11).
44 Hooker, *Ecclesiastical Polity*, V 57 (3).
45 Hooker, *Ecclesiastical Polity*, V 57 (4).
46 Hooker, *Ecclesiastical Polity*, V 57 (5).
47 Hooker, *Ecclesiastical Polity*, V 57 (6).
48 Hooker, *Ecclesiastical Polity*, V 57 (6).
49 Hooker, *Ecclesiastical Polity*, V 58 (1).
50 Hooker, *Ecclesiastical Polity*, V 58 (3).
51 Hooker, *Ecclesiastical Polity*, V 58 (3).
52 Leeming, *Principles of Sacramental Theology*, p 99.
53 Leeming, *Principles of Sacramental Theology*, p 99.
54 Leeming, *Principles of Sacramental Theology*, p 109.
55 Vonier, Anscar, *A Key to the Doctrine of the Eucharist*, p 31.
56 *ST*, III q 62 a 6.
57 Häring, Bernard, *The Law of Christ*, vol 2 p 151.
58 Häring, *The Law of Christ*, vol 2 p 151.
59 Zizioulas, John, *Being as Communion*, p 114.
60 Zizioulas, *Being as Communion*, p 117–18.
61 Zizioulas, *Being as Communion*, p 121.
62 Zizioulas, *Being as Communion*, p 121 n 26.
63 Pope Paul VI, *Opening Address to the second session of the Second Vatican Council*, 29 September 1963.

64 *Lumen Gentium*, 1 in Tanner & Alberigo, *Decrees*, vol 2 p 849.

65 *Lumen Gentium*, 11 in Tanner & Alberigo, *Decrees*, vol 2 p 857.

66 *Lumen Gentium*, 11, ibid.

67 *Lumen Gentium*, 11, ibid.

68 *Lumen Gentium*, 48 in Tanner & Alberigo, *Decrees*, vol 2 p 887.

69 Butler, Christopher, *The Theology of Vatican II*, p 136.

70 *Lumen Gentium*, 50 in Tanner & Alberigo, *Decrees*, vol 2 p 889.

3

Sacrifice

All those things called sacrifices are related to a particular true sacrifice
... some by way of counterpoint ... others announce the one true sacrifice
which needs be offered for sins; now that this sacrifice has been consum-
mated, Christians celebrate the memorial of it by the most holy oblation
and participation in the body and blood of Christ.[1]

S. Augustine of Hippo

CHRISTIAN SACRIFICE

The Christian doctrine of sacrifice takes its meaning not from
a general notion of religious cult applied to the circumstances
of the New Testament but from the oblation of the Son of God
on Calvary, anticipated by the sacrifices of the Old Covenant
and perpetuated in the sacramental mysteries celebrated by
the Church. Dom Anscar Vonier drew particular attention to
this in his own analysis of the Eucharistic sacrifice at a time
when the instinct of the Counter-Reformation to locate the
meaning of sacrifice in destruction was giving way to a new
definition which placed the essential meaning in the act of
sacred oblation.[2] Neither school appeared to preserve the unity
of the sacrifice of the Cross with its sacramental memorial in
the Eucharist: the former because it could not account successfully for the way in which the destruction of the victim took
place in the act of Eucharistic consecration; the latter because

53

it appeared to devise a further heavenly offering efficacious apart from that of Calvary. Vonier was anxious to retain both the scriptural and the sacramental dimensions of Christian sacrifice, and in doing so he recommends the reticence of S. Thomas Aquinas in dealing with oblation in a generic sense.

The Biblical concept of sacrifice illustrates a variety of rites, some with destruction of the offering and some without, which are exclusively reserved to the honour of God and which are endowed with a covenanted acceptance by him. Although the absence of interior repentance and a reliance on formalism in worship is castigated by the prophets of the Old Testament to the point that the entire efficacy of the cult is called into question, the sacramental principle remains: to exercise the virtue of religion even proleptically in the light of Christ's sacrifice, requires some external signification of the adoration and propitiation that elicits the sacred act. The Levitical association of blood with expiation and the remission of sin anticipates the sacrifice of the Cross and establishes the symbolic order in which that sacrifice will be perpetuated in an unbloody way in the Eucharist: the involuntary surrender of life by the sacrificial victims under the Law only has sacramental significance because their oblation is a covenanted anticipation of the voluntary surrender made by the Son to the Father on the Cross. In this voluntary surrender the interior act of religion, which is the distinguishing mark of true sacrifice, is made perfectly by the One who is both offering priest and sacrificial victim, the death of whom restores definitively the capacity of humankind to act as an authentically priestly people.

In her analysis of the rites which took place in the first Jerusalem Temple, Margaret Barker has brought into prominence the theme of priestly ritual atonement which informs the cultic setting of the Christian sacramental economy. Barker sees the Temple cult as a manifestation of the 'second' God in the person of the royal high priest, who undergoes a resurrection to a new angelic life through cultic participation with the divine in the Holy of Holies.[3] According to Barker the letter to the Hebrews explicitly identifies Melchizedek with this resurrected priesthood, in contrast with the purely legal status of the Aaronic priests: the restoration of the priesthood of Melchizedek to coincide with the covenantal renewal of the tenth Jubilee is therefore a key theme in the self-identification of Jesus Christ as he announces his ministry at Nazareth from the Jubilee text of Isaiah 61.[4] Furthermore, the royal high priest bore the name of the Lord on his forehead, and was therefore identified with him in his cultic actions, in particular when making atonement for sin: his ritual acts in the Temple, and in particular the reparative sacrifices which were offered to make atonement, were not simply the oblations of a human priest on behalf of his people; they were actions brought about and made effective by one who bore for this purpose the divine Name.[5]

This identification of the Lord as the priest who offers is complemented in the ritual of the Day of Atonement by his identification at the same time with the offering itself.[6] Vested in the angelic white vestments unique to the rite and the day, the High Priest enters the Holy of Holies where the offering of incense signifies the divine presence. Having offered the blood of a bull for his own sin, he then sacrifices the goat chosen by lot to bear the same name as the High Priest himself: that of the Lord. The blood of the goat is then sprinkled around the Holy of Holies and then on the Temple veil and the other cultic fittings of the sanctuary which in microcosm represents the created order to be reconciled to God. Meanwhile the second goat chosen to represent the fallen angel Azazel is driven out into the desert and killed, at which point the High Priest utters the divine name and the ritual is complete. Barker's thesis is of particular importance in articulating the presence in the Temple ritual as she reconstructs it of quite specific anticipations of the sacrificial work of Jesus Christ as priest and victim.

The complex substitution of the Atonement rite, in which through vesture, cultic setting and oblation the one who bore the divine Name offers a similarly designated sacrifice to restore the covenantal probity of the entire creation anticipates precisely the teaching of the letter to the Hebrews, in which Christ as High Priest terminates the repeated sacrifice with his own definitive self-offering secured by the ineluctable efficacy of his blood. To this Barker adds the communion shared by the priests made from the raw sacrifice mixed with sour wine, mentioned in the *Letter of Barnabas*: a communion unique as involving the consumption of blood, and which anticipates Christian ritual practice in the Eucharist.[7]

THE LOCATION OF CHRISTIAN SACRIFICE

The sacrifice of Christ on the Cross which Vonier describes as the normative oblation from which all the preceding rites take their meaning and purpose, is an offering which depends like that of the Day of Atonement on the shedding of blood. Vonier emphasises that because a true sacrifice is an act of Religion, and therefore a potential part of the virtue of Justice, it is essentially an objective rendering of what is due rather than a subjective exercise of fortitude in the face of extreme adversity or even death.[8] It is therefore not enough to say that the death of Christ on the Cross is a sacrifice because of the supreme obedience and self-emptying of the incarnate Word in accepting on behalf of sinners the destruction of his human life. Sacrifice is a ritual act, and the external sign which marks it as such is the handing over of the body as a substantive victim: to become as S. Paul says of Christ *a fragrant offering and sacrifice to God* (Eph. 5.2). The sacrifice is one of infinite worth because of the one who is both priest and victim, but it is neither the fortitude of the victim nor his dignity that makes the Cross sacrificial, it is the separation of his body and his blood.[9] Thomas Aquinas refers to Augustine to establish this *locus* of sacrifice in the flesh of Christ when he quotes him in defence of the sacrificial character of the Passion: *What could be so acceptably offered and accepted as the flesh of our sacrifice, which was made the body of our Priest?*[10]

The importance of this location of the sacrifice of Calvary in the flesh of Christ for S. Thomas is that it enables him to elucidate with clarity how the Passion is efficacious in just those ways which are not strictly an oblation. Thus the Passion when seen in relation to Christ's divinity seems to act in an efficient way, by causing our salvation; in relation to the human will of his soul in a meritorious way, by willingly submitting to the Cross; in relation to his flesh in a satisfactory way, by freeing us from punishment; in relation to freedom from guilt, by way of redemption; and in relation to reconciliation with God, by way of sacrifice. There is thus no state of sacrifice or actual exercise of the office of priest prior to the Passion as a simple consequence of the incarnation, deriving from the abnegation of the Word in taking flesh, his obedience to the Father in the undertaking of his ministry or indeed his institution of the Eucharist apart from the sacrifice of Calvary. These events and states of salvation history denote the holiness of the victim to be offered; they do not constitute the offering themselves. By making this distinction, it becomes possible to exclude from the strictly sacrificial character of the Passion of Christ all those elements which are variously essential for its consummation but which do not in themselves constitute sacrificial offering: the oblation consists in the visible, ritual act which separates the Lord's body and blood, ritual because in its dimensions and in its antecedents it conforms to the covenanted sacrificial economy it fulfils and ends. It is this location of the sacrifice in the separation of Christ's body and blood which enables the Eucharist to enjoy the character of a true and efficacious propitiatory sacrifice without detracting from the finality of the Passion.

THE EUCHARIST AS SACRIFICE

The identification of the Eucharist as the Christian sacrifice emerges in the patristic literature with Ignatius of Antioch and Justin Martyr, comes to fruition in all the principal theologians both Western and Eastern in the fourth century and remains generally unquestioned until the Reformation controversies provoke their violent reaction to the late scholastic consensus in the sixteenth century. Augustine is instrumental in articulating the classic understanding of the Eucharistic sacrifice, first by defining it as a sacramental sacrifice, and second by elucidating its character as an impetratory offering, effective for the well-being of both the living and the dead. Augustine's understanding of the Eucharist as a sacrifice is grounded in his theological analysis of a sacrament as a sacred sign, but also informed by an appeal to the practice of the Church in offering the oblation for particular intentions, and thus crucially not confining its application as a sacrament to those who actively participate in it.[11] Unlike the other sacraments, which are the covenanted applications of requisite grace to the appropriately disposed recipient by way of fitting sign, the Eucharist has from its character as a true and universal sacrifice a specific value in its celebration which benefits by way of suffrage those not physically present. This teaching is exemplified in a passage from his letter to Boniface which was to have an authoritative status in subsequent medieval thought: *Was not Christ once for all offered up in His own person as a sacrifice? And yet, is He not likewise offered up in the sacrament as a sacrament ... daily among our congregations ...? For if sacraments had not some point of resemblance to the things of which they are sacraments, they would not be sacraments at all.*[12]

This special character of the Eucharist as a sacrament which is both sacrament and sacrifice (not simply a sacrament and a sacrifice) is fundamental to the analysis which S. Thomas makes of its efficacy and application. It is the consecration

of bread and wine to be the body and blood of Christ
and therefore his presence under signs of separation which
constitute the sacrifice: it is the same sacrifice as Calvary, but
effected in an unbloody way and in an entirely distinct mode,
in which the exigencies of sacrifice in the order of nature play
no part.[13] Vonier emphasises in his discussion of this point
that the unbloody character of the Eucharistic sacrifice is not
simply the absence of gruesome detail and the concealment
of the suffering of the Passion behind, as it were, the discrete
veil of the Eucharistic species. Rather the sacrifice offered in
the Eucharist is one in which no physical death or destruction
occurs, precisely because it is a sacramental immolation and
not a natural one: the offering of Calvary is that of Christ
in propria specie, that of the Mass *in specie sacramenti*. There is
no hidden change in Christ himself brought about by the
offering of the Eucharistic sacrifice, no concealed destruction
or diminution which takes place in heaven when the oblation
is offered on earth. Rather, the dual consecration of the bread
and the wine makes Christ to be representatively present
under signs which realise sacramentally the victimhood of
Calvary.[14]

A HEAVENLY OFFERING?

This Thomist analysis of the Eucharistic sacrifice elucidated
by Vonier has been criticised for its lack of eschatological
reference and its exclusive emphasis on the death of Christ
as the *locus* of sacramental representation. In particular, it
appears to neglect the character of the Eucharist as an anticipation and foretaste of the heavenly worship, and excludes any
suggestion that in its offering there is a corresponding offering
made with and for the Church in heaven by the glorified
Christ.[15] Perhaps most coherently and influentially, the French
School of the seventeenth century in its consideration of the
priestly office sought a synthesis between the victimhood

of Christ in all his earthly states from the moment of his conception and the eternal exercise of his priesthood by way of adoration and intercession in heaven. The principal authors of the School did not shrink from the language of immolation, but in using it they sought to return the idea of sacrifice to what they considered to be an Augustinian emphasis on the internal reality of self-offering, rather than the outward cultic sign in itself. Thus for Charles de Condren, the act of sacrifice is completed only when in its consummation there is in heaven for all the elect *the eternal holocaust, which the divine fire of the Holy Spirit will consume without destroying on the altar of the divine Word, in the Temple of God, the bosom of the Father.*[16] Here the figure of Melchizedek as priest-adorer without death is of great significance: Jean-Jacques Olier asserted that *there is sacrifice in heaven, because heaven is most of all the place of perfect religion and of the highest worship that can be offered to God ... Our Lord, having been made a priest for all eternity according to the order of Melchizedek was constituted by God, his Father, to offer him sacrifice for ever.*[17]

The doctrine of the heavenly offering in the Eucharist received a new vigour in the twentieth century in the theology of the Anglican Charles Gore[18] and the Roman Catholic Maurice de la Taille,[19] although here without the distinctive emphasis on annihilation as the distinctive feature of interior sacrifice which led Condren to go as far as describing Christ's presence in heaven as being in a state of death. Gore identifies the sacrifice of the Church as being that of the material elements presented with praise and thanksgiving, together with the intercessions of the Church; these are made effective by incorporation into the heavenly offering of Christ which is the fruit of his passion and which continues for ever, though without a propitiatory character. De la Taille maintains the Tridentine identity of the Eucharistic sacrifice with that of the Cross, but locates the essential characteristic of sacrifice not in immolation, which is simply a necessary antecedent, but oblation. Thus the Eucharist offers Christ as glorified victim,

which in the light of its institution at the Last Supper effectively provides the Cross with its sacrificial context as ritual
oblation. This ritual oblation is begun by Christ at the Last
Supper, which the Cross completes by way of immolation and
which the Eucharist perpetuates as the presentation of the
now glorified victim; this without change to his person, but
recapitulating as now completed the entire sacrificial principle
which orientates his incarnate life.

Although perhaps more attractive devotionally than
the rather austere sacramental interpretation of sacrifice
exemplified by S. Thomas, the oblation-sacrifice school,
in seeking to avoid the inevitable concession to numerical
repetition involved in any destruction-sacrifice theory itself
falls into imprecision when it comes to determine in what
sense the offering of Calvary as a sacrifice is complete.
Vonier is conscious that the Eucharistic presence of Christ
is not confined to the body and blood as offered on the
Cross because the risen Christ is indivisible and always in
possession of all those states of his glorified humanity, which
the French School in particular realised are fundamental to
the formation of the Christian life in each communicant. But
he is able to emancipate these sacramental benefits from the
need to preserve the uniqueness of the sacrifice offered on
the Cross, not by attenuating the principle of sacrifice to an
interior attitude of oblation which exists in a most exemplary
way in the incarnate life of Christ lived as victim and priest,
but through the principle of concomitance.[20] This theological
principle, which is usually and regrettably associated with the
argument used at the Council of Trent to continue the practice
of refusing the Eucharistic cup to all but the celebrant at Mass,
has in fact a far more significant part to play in elucidating
the character of the Eucharist as being the sacrament which is
sacrament and sacrifice.

CONCOMITANCE AND SACRIFICE

Vonier establishes this point with immediate reference to the attributes of Christ as glorified: *The body and blood of Christ on the Christian altar are perfectly identical with the body and blood of Christ in heaven; therefore on the altar they are surrounded by all that surrounds them in the Person of Christ in heaven. But let us be very clear about this: this cortege of new splendours has nothing to do with the sacrament as such.*[21] This point is an expansion of that of Thomas Aquinas, who in answering the question as to whether the communion enjoyed by the disciples at the Last Supper was with the *impassible and glorious* Body of Christ states that: *Therefore the power of the sacramental words extends to this, that the body, i.e. Christ's, is under this sacrament, whatever accidents really exist in it.*[22] This concomitance has its archetype in the unity of substance but distinction of mission which obtains as a consequence of the incarnation of the divine Word: the Word becomes flesh but is not therefore divided from that perfect unity which is characteristic of the inward life of the divine Trinity; the body and blood of Christ are made present sacramentally in the Eucharistic elements by way of sacrifice, but are not thereby divorced from the concomitant glory of the integral glorified Saviour. Sacramental presence is effected by the performance of the rite (*vi sacramenti*) made intelligible by the appointed word (*vi verborum*). But through natural concomitance *there is also in this sacrament that which is really united with that thing wherein the aforesaid conversion is terminated ... For if any two things be really united, then wherever the one is really, there must the other also be: since things really united together are only distinguished by an operation of the mind.*[23] The heavenly intercession of Christ is therefore concomitant with the Eucharistic presence but not expressive of its character as sacrifice.

This distinction between the presence of Christ as sacrifice and his concomitant real presence in the fullness of his hypostatic union with all the glorified states of his human life, body and soul, is at least implicitly significant in the reappearance of sacrificial language about the Eucharist in Anglican theology after Hooker. Hooker himself was adamant in denying any sacrifice other than one of praise on the part of the participants in the Eucharist: reluctant even to use the word 'priest' because of its sacrificial connotations, he asserts *sacrifice is now no part of Church ministry*.[24] However, given the distinctive English reformation indifference to defining the manner of Christ's presence in the Eucharist, so long as transubstantiation is excluded, it is significant to see how rapidly both the language of sacrifice and the cultic appurtenances in ritual and architecture were generated by the Laudian movement out of the inherited Elizabethan raw material of Prayer Book and Ordinal. Writing in his controversy with Cardinal Perron, Lancelot Andrewes declared: *If we agree about the matter of the Sacrifice, there will be no difference about the Altar. The Holy Eucharist being considered as a Sacrifice (in the representation of the Breaking of the Bread and pouring forth of the Cup), the same is fitly called an Altar; which again is fitly called a Table, the Eucharist being considered as a sacrament, which is nothing else but a distribution and an application of the Sacrifice to the several believers.*[25] Andrewes' association of sacrifice with death is so emphatic that he describes the invitation of the Christian to communion as being an invitation to come to the corpse of Christ.[26]

However, this sacrificial interpretation of the Eucharistic action in Anglicanism was not confined to the representational theory of oblation; contemporaneously with the thought of the French School, the identity of the Eucharistic sacrifice with the exercise of Christ's priesthood in heaven becomes prominent in the work of Jeremy Taylor. He wrote in his Life of Christ of 1649 (itself a Berullean project): *There He sits, a High Priest continually, and offers still the same one perfect Sacrifice; that is, still represents it as having been once finished and consummate, in order to perpetual and never failing events. And this also his ministers do on earth. They offer up the same sacrifice to God, the Sacrifice of the*

Cross by prayers, and a commemorating rite and representment, according to his holy institution ... Our very holding up of the Son of God and representing Him to His Father is the doing an act of mediation and advantage to ourselves in the virtue and efficacy of the Mediator.[27] Taylor does not accept transubstantiation, and he locates the sacrificial ministry of Christ clearly in the heavenly offering and not in the sacramental signification of his death. But because he grasps the character of the Eucharist as being sacrificial in its most proper sense, he is able to assert an offering which is mediatory, advantageous and efficacious for those on whose behalf the appointed ministry of the Church offers it. However, this distinctive combination of an objective and meritorious sacrifice in the Eucharist without a correspondingly robust exegesis of the real presence was insufficient to sustain itself as normative in the restored cultic economy of 1662.

SACRIFICE AND PRESENCE

What sort of sacramental presence in the Eucharistic elements is needed to sustain the sacrificial character of the Eucharist if a simply representational model does not achieve this? In his discussion of transubstantiation, Dom Vonier emphasises that the sacramental reality takes precedence over the means by which we understand it to be accomplished, and that the pre-eminent Eucharistic truth is that the body and blood of Christ are given to us *in* the form of sacrifice. Transubstantiation properly understood after the mind of S. Thomas and according to what was defined at the Council of Trent describes the divine act whereby what is indicated in the words of consecration comes to be in the elements consecrated. There is no symbolic or sacramental correspondence between the fact of such a change and the ritual presentation of the victim for sacrifice, nor any multiplication of Christ's presence in many places in addition to his heavenly session, which the Black Rubric in *The Book of Common Prayer* quite justly states is *against the truth of Christ's natural body to be at one time in more places than one.* This Thomas Aquinas elucidates when he says: *Hence we say that Christ's body is upon many altars, not as in different places, but* sacramentally; *and thereby we do not understand that Christ is there only as in a sign, although a sacrament is a kind of sign; but that Christ's body is here after a fashion proper to this sacrament.*[28] The sacramental character of this presence is so fundamental that the end of the means by which the representational signification is accomplished is also the end of the sacramental presence: *in this way God simply ceases to be the Lord of a creature which ceases to exist.*[29]

It is this objective sacramental change which makes the Eucharist distinctive not only in its character as a sacrifice but in its operation as a sacrament. The other sacramental rites are completed through the use of the material sign to efficaciously convey grace, whereas in the Eucharist the rite is perfected in the consecration of the matter itself; likewise, in the other sacraments the consecration of the matter to be used is by way of blessing, whereas in the Eucharist it effects a real change which makes actual the designation as body and blood determined by the formula of consecration.[30] This presence however is one which is properly and exclusively sacramental: it is not a disguise for the natural state of Christ's now glorified body, nor according to S. Thomas is it a presence as important (*potior*) as his human presence in its natural state, hence the formal character of the reverence paid to the sacrament when reserved, carried about or otherwise used in relation to the rites of the Church.[31] But unlike the purely representational character of the sacrament envisaged by Andrewes and Taylor, in which the substantial outward signs of bread and wine relate to their spiritual antitype of the sacrificed body and blood much as the water of Baptism relates to the infusion of the Holy Spirit, the Thomist account of the real presence can account for the reality of the sacramental sacrifice prior to the reception of the Eucharistic gifts by those who will communicate. This gives it the objective character it needs if it is to be what Taylor does not hesitate to call *an act of mediation and advantage* of itself.

THE EUCHARIST AS IMPETRATORY

If the oblation of the Eucharist does not then depend on the participation of the communicants who are present, how does it benefit those who are absent? An understanding of the Eucharist which envisages it being celebrated for the good of the whole Church both living and departed, and as having a particular impetrative value beyond that of the usual practice of public intercession for particular intentions, is the chief practical consequence of conceiving it as a sacramental sacrifice. Nor is this principle one which has its origins simply in the late medieval multiplication of and commodification of rites which both the Reformation and the Counter-Reformation repudiated as a distortion of perceived primitive simplicity. The usage of offering the Eucharist for a particular individual's benefit is mentioned by both S. Cyprian and Tertullian,[32] and this designation could be applied to the dead as well as to the living, provided always that in both cases the bond of communion with the Church in life was present. Augustine encouraged his priests to offer the Eucharist for particular intentions, on one occasion to deliver a household from demonic infestation, and he enlarges his theology of intercession for the departed by appealing to the practice he names as apostolic of offering the Eucharist and giving alms for the repose of the pious dead.[33] This Augustinian synthesis becomes the normative practice of the Latin Church through the moral theology of Pope S. Gregory the Great: the sacrifice is efficacious for the living because in evoking the passion of the Lord on our behalf it makes a representative immolation with the absolving power of the original for both the living and the departed.[34]

The stability of this teaching in the rites of Eucharistic celebration is shown by the invariable practice of including intercession in the Eucharistic prayer itself. One of the most significant practical consequences of the rejection of the notion of sacrifice in the Eucharist at the Reformation was the exclusion of these prayers for the living and the departed from what remained of the various revisions and replacements of the Roman Canon made at that time. In response to this rejection, the Latin theological tradition developed a theory of fruits in the Eucharistic celebration, which sought to distinguish how the Eucharist could be at once the sacramental sacrifice of the Cross entire in itself, but also efficacious in a particular sense when applied to a particular person, object or intention. The eclipse of this immense casuistry in recent years has not in fact obscured the fundamental insight that the Eucharist is of benefit to those for whom it is offered, an insight which is variously preserved both in the splendid rhetoric of Gregory Dix's *Was ever another command so obeyed*[35] and in the more prosaic reality of the mass stipend economy which still obtains in much of Catholic Europe. The power and efficacy of the Cross is infinite for the forgiveness of sins and the restoration of the life of grace in humankind; the sacramental participation of the Church in that infinite sacrifice is necessarily finite, because it pertains to a given moment, and so is susceptible to a finite application.

EUCHARIST AND COMMUNION

S, Thomas Aquinas states as the abiding principle of sacramental theology that the sacraments are given for the use of humankind, and that use in the case of the Eucharistic sacrifice must evidently culminate in the fact of sacramental communion, even if the fruitfulness of the oblation for the good of the Church and the world has a value simply in the completed act of consecration itself.[36] That the communion of the priest who celebrates is necessary for the integrity of the rite is reflected in the universal practice of the Latin and Eastern liturgies, is confirmed by the teaching of the Council of Trent and is maintained by the rubrical directions of the various Anglican liturgies of the early modern period despite different practice in the other reformed communities. This follows from the representative congruity which obtains in the rite: as its celebration is a representative image of the Passion, so the altar is a representative image of the Cross and the priest the representative image of the Christ who offers himself.

It has been the particular insight of the great reaction from Jansenism since the seventeenth century in the West, first in moral theology and then in liturgical practice, that a sacramental economy which assumes a largely non-communicating laity is an inadequate expression of the way in which, as Henri de Lubac put it, for the first millennium the Eucharist made the Church.[37] The consequences of this change have been immense, because they have effectively overturned a pattern of Christian practice which is first apparent in the regret of S. John Chrysostom that so many of the Christians of Antioch abstained from holy communion out of fear,[38] and which remained significant until the pastoral reforms of S. Pius X in 1905.

The fundamental communion that the Church possesses and maintains with Christ her head, and the character that the people of God receive as a royal priesthood through adoption into Christ's high priesthood is Eucharistic: *The cup of blessing which we bless, is it not a sharing in the blood of Christ? The bread that we break, is it not a sharing in the body of Christ? Because there is but one bread, we who are many are one body, for we all partake of the one bread* (1 Cor. 10.16). This integrative character of the act of sacramental communion derives from the manner of Christ's presence: in the consecration of the bread and wine to be his body and blood, his presence is multiplied without him being multiplied; in the act of communion, our multiplicity is re-integrated into the unity of the Christ who is head and life of the body. The insightful Eucharistic theologian Charles Journet calls this presence of the mystical body in the celebration of the Mass *the signified in the sign, and the effect in the cause.*[39] This is because the sacramental act of Eucharistic consecration and communion creates the ecclesial body but does not itself contain it: rather the sacramental presence and participation of Christ constitutes the Church as its greatest good. This instinct is found in Augustine's conception of the Eucharistic unity of the Church: *Such is the sacrifice of Christians: to be all one body in Jesus Christ, and it is this mystery that the Church celebrates in the sacrament of the altar where she learns to offer herself in the oblation which she makes to God.*[40]

The covenanted gift of grace which sacramental participation communicates to each Christian is as various in its individual effect as the dispositions of those who receive it, but the outward signification of the body and blood by bread and wine articulates the overall purpose of the sacrament as sustenance in the spiritual life, unity in the body and the gift of life by the forgiveness of sin. These purposes are well summed up by the conclusion of the Council of Trent on the reasons for the institution of the Eucharist: *He wishes this sacrament to be taken as the spiritual food of souls, to nourish and strengthen them as they lived by his life who said he who eats me will live because of me, and as an antidote to free us from daily faults and preserve us from mortal sins. He further wished it to be a pledge of our future glory and unending happiness, and thus a sign of that one body of which he is head, and to which he wished us all to be united by the closest bonds of faith, hope and love.* There is thus in the Eucharist food for the journey which endows the Christian with Christ's life; a remedy for sin which derives from the character of the one sacrifice it commemorates; an eschatological anticipation of the glory of heaven which complements the sacramental signification of Christ as sacrificed with a real concomitance of his life as divine and glorified; and a sign and aspiration of that unity between all in communion which the Council defines as instituted here *in order that we might all have the same sentiment and that there might be no division among us.*[41]

The strict Thomist view that the sacrifice in the Eucharist pertains to the sacramental signification of Christ's death on Calvary and not to any local manifestation of his supposed priestly self-offering in heaven is reflected in Catherine Pickstock's consideration of Eucharistic participation as an economy of dispossession.[42] To celebrate the Eucharist and to participate in Christ as he is made present in the rite sacramentally is to be literally obedient to death: by receiving Christ as offered in a sacrificial mode we do indeed proclaim the Lord's death until he comes again by our own conformity to his expiatory act of priestly oblation. In doing so the Eucharistic Christian not only participates in the one true sacrifice which gives meaning to all those which pre-figured it under the Law, but also reiterates the Abrahamic sacrifice of faith, which by not turning from death receives authentic life. Because this participation takes place within a finite and temporal setting, one in which human sin continues to impede and extinguish the work of divine grace, the celebration of the Eucharist and the gift of Christ in sacramental communion needs to be repeated as often as the benefits of the redemption are applied: S. Thomas says, *Now since, owing to our daily defects, we stand in daily need of the fruits of our Lord's Passion, this sacrament is offered regularly every day in the Church.*[43] Although insofar as he compares the Eucharist with the other sacraments he locates its sacrificial accomplishment in the word and act of consecration, not the communion which follows, yet in considering how Christians are conformed to the expiatory oblation of the Cross and fed with Christ himself in the rite, Aquinas is willing to say that *In the New Law, the true sacrifice of Christ is presented to the faithful under the form of bread and wine.*[44]

THE INTEGRITY OF THE CHRISTIAN SACRIFICE

Christianity is a religion of sacrifice because it is established by the redemptive sacrifice of the Cross: the sacrificial cult of the Temple anticipates this one substantive atonement and gives it its ritual context; the celebration of the Eucharist perpetuates it by way of memorial, and applies its infinite worth to the finite eventualities of the Body of Christ which by the bond of sacramental communion it constitutes and effects. In itself the Eucharistic sacrifice is not a perpetuation of the sacrifice of the Cross by evoking on earth a symbolic representation of Christ's heavenly intercession: its sacrificial significance is confined to the ritual act which consecrates bread and wine separately to be the Lord's body and blood. However, by the power and congruity of concomitance Christ in all his mysteries is present, even if by virtue of what is integral to the sacramental sacrifice he is present simply as body and blood. The exclusion of any sense of hidden immolation in the Eucharist, whether through a prolongation of Christ's self-oblation in heaven or by some new curtailment or annihilation of his glorified state through submission to consecration under material signs, preserves the fundamentally sacramental character of the Christian sacrifice. It is an unbloody offering: instituted as such at the Last Supper and so quite different in its mode of offering from the sacrifice of Calvary, even though identical to it with respect to the victim offered, the priest who offers and the efficacy of its fruitfulness.

If then the Christian moral life is given its orientation to beatitude in a cultic mode by the virtue of religion, then the offering of the Eucharist will be the culminating sacramental act of that cult, and the one which realises not only the corporate designation of the Church as royal and priestly by Christ her head, but which also integrates and nourishes each individual Christian through the act of sacramental communion. Here even if the sacrifice so represented has in

71

itself no specifically eschatological reference, the presence and gift of Christ himself in the fullness of his glorified humanity acts as a pledge of future glory and eternal happiness. But the cultic character of the Eucharistic sacrifice at the summit of the sacramental economy means that it is emphatically not a ritual practice whose origin and efficacy can be confined to those gathered at a particular celebration. The application of the sacrifice of Calvary by way of suffrage for the whole Church in all its various needs encompasses not simply the absent living but also the dead who rest in Christ, as the intercessory character of the classic Eucharistic prayers of both East and West demonstrates. Participation in the Eucharistic mystery has never been confined either theologically or historically to those able to play an active part in the gathered assembly. The sacrificial character of the Eucharist gives to its celebration a prior authenticity in manifesting the whole atoning act of Christ in a local setting with respect to both place and time: the sacramental communion that follows from this is in its individual benefit *varied as the heart of man*,[45] but in its objective value the grace-filled incursion of beatitude into the ritual act which pleads for it.

Notes for Chapter 3

1 Augustine, *Answer to Faustus, a Manichaean*, 20.18.
2 Vonier, Anscar, *A Key to the Doctrine of the Eucharist*, pp 104–115.
3 Barker, Margaret, *Temple Theology: An Introduction*, pp 53–73.
4 Barker, *Temple Theology*, p 72.
5 Barker, *Temple Theology*, pp 58–60.
6 Barker, *Temple Theology*, p 61.
7 Barker, *Temple Theology*, p 69.
8 *It is not the heroic fortitude of Christ on the Cross which constitutes the sacrifice, but the material fact ... of the pouring out of his blood*, Vonier, *Key*, p 108.
9 *Now Christ's death is the separation of his Body and Blood; we do neither more nor less when we sacrifice at the altar*, Vonier, *Key*, p 73
10 *ST*, III q 48 a 3.
11 Augustine, *Enchiridion* 110.
12 Augustine, *Letter 98* to Bishop Boniface.
13 *Sacrifice in sacramento is not merely an attenuated, a mild form of the natural sacrifice; the two have nothing in common except the divine Victim which is being immolated*, Vonier, *Key*, p 59.
14 *Such, then, is the content of the Eucharistic sacrament. Christ in the state of Victim before God, His Body and Blood a sacrifice of sweet savour to the Lord.* Vonier, *Key*, p 87.
15 A criticism made by Aidan Nichols OP in his introduction to Vonier, *Key*, p xiv
16 Condren, Charles de, The Eternal Sacrifice, p 179.
17 Olier, Jean-Jacques, *L'Esprit des cérémonies de la messe: explication des cérémonies de la grand'messe de paroisse selon l'usage romaine*, given in O'Collins, Gerald and Jones, Michael, *Jesus our Priest* p 193.
18 Gore, Charles, The Body of Christ
19 De la Taille, Maurice, *Mysterium Fidei, de augustissimo corporis et sanguinis Christi sacrificio et sacramento*.
20 Vonier, *Key*, pp 136–46.

21 Vonier, *Key*, p 137.
22 *ST*, III q 81 a 3.
23 *ST*, III q 76 a 1.
24 Hooker, Richard, *Ecclesiastical Polity*, V 78 (2).
25 See More, Paul, & Cross, F Leslie, *Anglicanism. The Thought and Practice of the Church of England, illustrated from the religious Literature of the Seventeenth Century*, p 497.
26 *Not He alone, But He as at the very act of his offering is made present to us … we must repair even* ad cadaver, Andrewes, Lancelot, *Sermons of the Resurrection* vii, see Gore, *Body of Christ*, p 183 n 1.
27 Taylor, Jeremy, *The Great Exemplar of Sanctity and Holy Life according to the Christian Institution in the History of the Life and Death of the ever blessed Jesus Christ the Saviour of the World*, 3.15.
28 *ST*, III q 75 a 1.
29 *ST*, III q 76 a 6.
30 *ST*, III q 80 a 12.
31 Vonier, *Key*, p 133–4.
32 See Stone, Darwell, *A History of the Doctrine of the Holy Eucharist*, vol 1 pp 46–8.
33 Augustine, *City of God* 22.8; *Enchiridion* 110.
34 Gregory the Great, *Dialogues*, 4.58–60.
35 Dix, Gregory, *The Shape of the Liturgy*, p 744.
36 *ST*, III q 78 a 1.
37 See especially De Lubac, Henri, *Corpus Mysticum: The Eucharist and the Church in the Middle Ages*, pp 13–36.
38 Chrysostom, John, *Homilies on the Epistle to the Ephesians*, Cap 4 Homily 11.
39 Journet, Charles, *The Mass: the Presence of the Sacrifice of the Cross*, p 186.
40 Augustine, *City of God*, 10.6.
41 Council of Trent, *Decree on the Most Holy Sacrament of the Eucharist*, Session 13. Chapter 2 in Tanner & Alberigo, Decrees, vol 2 p 694.
42 Pickstock, Catherine, *After Writing*, pp 238–52.
43 *ST*, III q 83 a 2.
44 *ST*, III q 22 a 6.
45 Aquinas, *Sequence for Corpus Christi*, transl. J M Neale.

4

Priesthood

The sacraments of the New Law produce a character, in so far as by them we are deputed to the worship of God according to the rite of the Christian religion.[1]

Thomas Aquinas

THE PRIESTHOOD OF JESUS CHRIST

The fundamental priesthood which humankind is able to exercise before God is that of Jesus Christ. His person and work are definitive in showing what priesthood is, just as his Passion is definitive in showing what sacrifice is. The ministry of the levitical priesthood anticipates that of Christ just as the sacrifices of the Temple anticipate the sacramental economy of the Church, but this anticipation is not comprehensive, as the appeal to the figure of Melchizedek in the letter to the Hebrews makes clear. Indeed, it is this letter which provides the only account in the New Testament of the role of Jesus as priest by name, and it is a priesthood at once fulfilling what has gone before and yet radically superseding it. It is the case that other New Testament writings identify in an unsystematic way themes which come to particular prominence in this letter: thus the letter to the Romans speaks of Christ interceding for us at the right hand of the Father (Rom. 8.34); the letters to the Colossians and the Ephesians mention the same heavenly session (Col. 3.1; Eph. 1.20); and the identification of Christ with the Lord of Ps. 110 occurs in 1 Cor. 15.25 and in all three synoptic gospels in the context of Jesus' question to the Pharisees about his divine sonship. However, the word 'priest' itself only occurs in the letter to the Hebrews with reference to Jesus (six times simply as priest and ten times as high priest): the cultic language and practice of the Temple are invoked and then re-cast in the light of the unique character of the sacrifice offered and the one who makes it.

What is distinctive about this new and normative priesthood, which belongs to the one who is *a merciful and faithful high priest in the service of God ... to make a sacrifice of atonement for the sins of the people* (Heb. 2.17)? First, the sacrifice offered is unique and unrepeated, because unlike the expiatory sacrifices of animals which preceded it, it is absolutely efficacious and in need of no substantive repetition to maintain its vigour: *this he did once for all, when he offered himself* (Heb. 7.27). This completed character of the sacrifice does not exclude the continuing heavenly intercession of the one who offered it, but this is not the perpet-uation of the sacrifice in a different mode. The entitlement to offer this sacrifice of propitiation to God is problematic in terms of the Temple system of cult on two grounds: first, the one offering himself is not entitled to be called priest because he is not of the priestly tribe of Levites to whom this office exclusively pertains; and second, the sacrifice is offered not in the designated place of cult which is the Temple and its altar, but as the letter describes it *outside the city gate* (Heb. 13.12), in a profane place of execution. By way of apology for the authen-ticity and indeed priority of Christ's priesthood the author of the letter to the Hebrews establishes first the integrity of his humanity in common with us (1.14); his appointment by God to this office (5.5–6); and his aptness as victim proved by fidelity (5.8–9) and designated by *the eternal Spirit* (9.14) as an unblemished offering to the Father.

AFTER THE ORDER OF MELCHIZEDEK

The victimhood of Christ as this unblemished offering is explained in a cultic context by paschal signification in Paul (1 Cor. 5.7) and the gospel of John (1.29, 36; 19.31, 36) and by atonement signification in Paul (Rom. 3.25) and in the ninth chapter of the letter to the Hebrews. But fundamental to the authenticity of Christ's high priesthood to the writer to the Hebrews is his prior identification as priest with Melchizedek, the elusive priest-king of Salem to whom Abraham pays tithe and whose offering is bread and wine (Gen. 14.17–20). The ostensible force of this argument it that Melchizedek is a priest who precedes the Levitical priesthood in time and so in priority; whose office is reverenced by Abraham as higher than his own by payment of tithe and so more dignified than any which might be appointed later from his own progeny; and who by virtue of his want of genealogy possesses an eternal ministry, *Without father, without mother, without genealogy, having neither beginning of days nor end of life, but resembling the Son of God, he remains a priest for ever* (Heb. 7.3). This priesthood is furthermore guaranteed by the divine oath of Ps. 110.4 in a way which the Levitical priesthood never enjoys: *the Lord has sworn and will not change his mind, you are a priest for ever, according to the order of Melchizedek*. Although the act of atonement by which the sacrifice of the Cross delivers humankind from sin is the consummation of this priesthood, nevertheless the letter to the Hebrews emphasises how the fact of the incarnation itself, and the faithful obedience of Christ in his earthly life without sin both hidden and public, designate him as the authentic high priest of the new covenant, even if this fidelity to the Father's will is not in itself the expiatory oblation.

Is the figure of Melchizedek as a priest like the son of God more fundamental to the understanding of Jesus' person and ministry than the immediate evidence of the letter to the Hebrews might suggest? His presence as the *summus sacerdos* in the Canon of the Roman Mass[2] develops the character of his priesthood from the status of his person to his offering of bread and wine, which are naturally symbolic of the Eucharistic oblation to come. The work of Margaret Barker has drawn particular attention to the importance attached to the person and role of Melchizedek in the Melchizedek scroll from Qumran: here he is a messianic figure whose re-appearance at the time of the tenth Jubilee was to make the final and definitive atonement sacrifice.[3] His priesthood, obscured by the problematic Hebrew of Ps. 110, is one of resurrection, the cultic re-birth through entry into the holy of holies whereby the royal priest of the first Temple came to be a proleptic incarnation of the Lord, the 'second' God. Like Melchizedek, the priesthood of Jesus is one which is authenticated not by descent from the hieratic line of Aaron, but by ascent, the resurrection which imparts to the one raised an indestructible priesthood.

CHRIST'S PRIESTHOOD AND EUCHARIST

If the letter to the Hebrews articulates a doctrine of Christ's priesthood which designates him as divinely appointed, consecrated by the Spirit to atone by virtue of his fidelity and definitively efficacious in the act of atonement itself, then the accounts of the Last Supper in the synoptic gospels provide the ritual setting for the sacrificial meal by which the high priest is to perpetuate the memory of the offering he is about to make. The institution of the Eucharist at the Last Supper takes place within the cultic setting of the Passover, and establishes in its place a new ritual commemoration of the covenant of God with humankind, one which is evidently already fundamental to the sacramental economy of the nascent Church by the time Paul has cause to write about abuses in its celebration to the Corinthians. How can the Last Supper institute the commemoration of an offering that is still to be made? Thomas Aquinas follows Innocent III in asserting that in the consecrated bread and wine of the Last Supper Christ *bestowed on the disciples his body such as it was.*[4] There is no anticipation of the impassible resurrection body: although Christ as sacramentally present has no extension in space and so cannot experience the various incidents of the Passion visited upon him *in proprio specie*, yet had the sacramental presence first instituted at the Last Supper endured during the Passion, there would have been an actual separation of body and blood under the species of bread and wine, and no concomitant presence of Christ's human soul once it was divided from his body by death.

The alternative view which S. Thomas finds in Hugh of St Victor and which characterizes the approach of the Anglican Charles Gore[5] is that the presence of Christ in the Eucharistic communion of the Last Supper is impassible and glorious by way of anticipation, just as at the Transfiguration a similar anticipation of the state of glory took place, and after the resurrection by contrast Christ though in no strict need of it submitted to the needs of mortal living by eating and drinking. Thomas denies this by reiterating that the body of Christ given in the Last Supper must be the body then perceptible to the disciples: possible with respect to its readiness to undergo the Passion, impassible only insofar as its dimensive state governed by the accidents of bread and wine excluded the infliction of suffering on that body *sub specie sacramentis*. However, even if the character of Christ's sacramental presence at the Last Supper is not an anticipation of the glorification of his human nature at the resurrection, the institution of the rite by which the sacrifice of the Cross will be commemorated is an anticipation of the atonement which this sacrifice will accomplish. Moreover the rite in itself is not one which anticipates a bloody sacrifice through any external resemblance: there is nothing in the Last Supper which by virtue of the act of celebrating it symbolises Calvary. Instead its efficacy as a remembrance comes from its sacramental setting in a cultic rite, the rite of the Passover which designates Jesus Christ as the sacrificial Lamb and which constitutes the memorial of his death as a new and eternal covenant with salvific effect for all.

The Johannine writings contain no explicit narrative of the institution of the Eucharist but instead expound the ministry of Jesus as priest first in terms of his self-identification as the Bread of Life which is given as a sacrifice and second as a victim willingly consecrated to the will of the Father: *I am the living bread that came down from heaven. Whoever eats of this bread will live for ever; and the bread that I will give for the life of the world is my flesh* (Jn 6.51*)*. The purpose of the incarnation of the Word is to take human flesh, but this flesh is orientated towards immolation from the beginning, in order that by its own destruction it might give life to the world. Jesus is identified as the instigator of a new and perfect cult in the Temple of his own body (Jn 2.22), one in which the designated holy place of the old ritual will give way to a priestly intercession offered from the sanctuary of his own glorified body. In particular, this priestly self-offering takes its context from the setting of the Passover, both the sacrifice of the lamb and the commemoration of the miracle of the feeding: Jesus is designated as the Lamb of God by John at the beginning of his ministry, to be consummated by his death at the moment of the Passover sacrifice (Jn 19.14, 31); his miraculous recapitulation of the gift of manna in anticipation of the bread of life takes place at the same season (Jn 6.4). This priestly designation finds its explicit expression in the seventeenth chapter of the gospel, in which immediately before his Passion Jesus consecrates himself for sacrifice before the Father on behalf of those to whom he has been sent: *And for their sakes I sanctify myself, so that they also may be sanctified in truth* (Jn 17.19).

The priesthood of Jesus Christ is therefore one which has in common with the levitical priesthood the offering of blood, but which is superior to this priesthood in a way which the figure of Melchizedek exemplifies and anticipates, because what the priest-king of Salem offers symbolically is bread and wine which at the Last Supper are made substantially the sacramental sacrifice by which the Church is unified and fed with the fruits of the Passion.[6] Christ's sacrifice on the Cross is a complete atonement, never to be repeated and standing in no need of any completion, sacramental or otherwise: the fidelity in the flesh which makes this atonement acceptable begins at the first moment of the incarnation, but this consecration is not the oblation itself, nor is the perseverance of Christ's priesthood in heaven and his intercession there any continuation of the oblation which is complete on Calvary. The exercise of this priesthood in offering himself as victim on the Cross for the redemption of sin is a ritual act, and by a ritual act is perpetuated in the sacramental sacrifice of the Eucharist; concomitant with the death of the victim is the act of perfect worship which accompanies the shedding of blood, and which although not in itself sacrificial is meritorious in demonstrating the perfect fidelity and humility of Christ as priest, who thus is raised to life in glory. It is this priesthood of Christ that is perpetuated in the Church, first by the designation of all the baptised as a priestly people, and second by the exercise of ministerial priesthood by those so ordained.

THE PRIESTHOOD OF THE BAPTISED

The priesthood which belongs to the Church is described in particular in the first letter of Peter: Christ the *living stone* becomes the foundation of a *spiritual house* which is the home of a *holy priesthood* (1 Pet. 2.4, 9). This priesthood offers *spiritual sacrifices* (2.5) which are acceptable to God through the mediation of Jesus Christ: these consist of singing the *mighty acts of him who called you out of darkness into his wonderful light* (1 Pet. 2.9), and produce good works which edify the pagans (1 Pet. 2.12). This language of spiritual sacrifice offered by a priestly people reflects both the covenantal priestly designation made in Exodus 19.6 and the transposition of sacrificial language into an ethical and interior commitment to repentance and good works found in several of the psalms. This corporate identification of the Church as holy and able to offer acceptable sacrifice through the mediation of its head is present also in Revelation, in which Christ is designated as the Lamb of sacrifice and the people whom he has redeemed through this efficacious victimhood as *a kingdom, priests serving his God and Father* (Rev. 1.6). The setting of the heavenly liturgy and the cult practices which are associated with it such as the offering of incense are intentionally redolent of the worship of the Temple: within this archetypal Temple, the martyred saints intercede from beneath the altar (Rev. 6.9–11), themselves being sacrificial first-fruits redeemed by the Lamb (Rev. 14.4).

The letters of Paul similarly employ priestly language to describe the Christian life, principally in the ethical sense of spiritual sacrifice. The letter to the Romans concludes with the exhortation to *present your bodies as a living sacrifice, holy and acceptable to God, which is your spiritual worship* (Rom. 12.1), which gives a cultic orientation to the moral quality of Christian living. This cultic language also attaches to the good works of Christian communities on Paul's behalf: the collection for the Church in Jerusalem is described as an act of *leitourgia* (2 Cor. 9.12), and the support of the Philippians for Paul himself is called *a fragrant offering, a sacrifice acceptable and pleasing to God* (Phil. 4.18). Paul uses of his own ministry sacrificial language appropriate to a priestly offering when he describes the prospect of his imminent condemnation: *I am being poured out as a libation over the sacrifice and the offering of your faith* (Phil. 2.17). Most strikingly, Paul describes himself as a 'liturgist' *of Christ Jesus to the gentiles in the priestly service of the gospel of God, so that the offering of the gentiles may be acceptable, sanctified by the Holy Spirit* (Rom. 15.15–6). Here the work of evangelisation is expressed in priestly terms, in which Paul's work adds to the number of God's people, and so enables the true worship of holy lives to be offered just as the Temple priesthood worked to sanctify Israel. The language of priesthood found in the New Testament which refers to Christians therefore has a two-fold register: first, it is a designation of covenantal holiness, which enables acceptable worship to be offered to God through the mediation of Christ; and second, it is a transposition of the language of sacrifice into an ethical mode, in which all works which tend to the extension of the kingdom have a cultic character in the Christian moral life.

MINISTERIAL PRIESTHOOD

The process by which the title of priest becomes attached to those Christian ministers who in virtue of their ordination celebrate the Eucharist begins in the sub-apostolic period and is complete by the fourth century in both East and West.[7] The extent to which this development has established itself as the norm by this time is demonstrated by the paradoxical rhetoric which S. Gregory Nazianzus employs in writing to his friend bishop Amphilochius: *Do not cease, pious man, to pray and intercede for me, when you draw down the Logos through the word, when you sacrifice the body and blood of the Lord with unbloody cut through the sharpness of your word.*[8] This process can be seen at work in S. Ignatius, who calls the location in which the Eucharist is offered a place of sacrifice, and with Clement of Rome, who invites a comparison of the three-fold Christian ministry of bishop, priest and deacon with that of the Temple hierarchy.[9] In the West both Tertullian and S. Cyprian identify the bishop as the principal cultic officiant in the Church: Tertullian calls him *summus sacerdos* to indicate that the presbyters too are entitled to the title in its simple form, while Cyprian uses *sacerdos* to indicate cultic functions and *episcopus* to indicate those pertaining to governance.[10] In the East the usage is found in the Apostolic Constitutions which refers to the bishops and other priests, and in Cyril of Jerusalem, who relates the word specifically to the celebration of the Eucharist.

The golden age of patristic literature in the fourth century produced many treatises on the dignity and duties of the Christian priesthood which take as established both the permanence of the character it endows and the cultic delegation which forms a principal part of its responsibilities. This is the case both in the East with the seminal treatise of S. John Chrysostom *On the Priesthood* and the more autobiographical *Apologia pro fuga sua* of S. Gregory Nazianzus, and in the West with the Ciceronian *De Officis Ministrorum* of S. Ambrose and the definitive exegesis of the pastoral office made by S. Gregory the Great in the *Cura Pastoralis*. These texts demonstrate that in defining the offices of the episcopate and presbyterate as priestly by virtue of the celebration of the Eucharist, no derogation was being made from the pastoral and didactic responsibilities integral to the Christian ministry as the New Testament conceived it, nor from the essentially vocational character of the call to exercise such a ministry. The principle of ministerial character – that is, the indelibility of ordination when validly conferred regardless of the sinfulness or heresy of the ordaining bishop or candidate – emerges from the circumstances of the Donatist controversy and finds its first systematic expression in Augustine: he calls the ministerial character *ordinis ecclesiae signaculum*, an indelible designation by God which makes all subsequent sacramental ministrations performed by the priest authentic because of they belong not to him but to God Himself.

The patristic account of the character of holy order demonstrates a consensus shared between the Latin and Greek portions of the Church about certain fundamentals: the sacrificial character of the Eucharist makes the language of priesthood appropriate to describe those to whom its celebration is reserved, primarily the bishop but also by delegation the presbyters as *sacerdotes secundi ordinis*, whose enhanced pastoral responsibilities for churches apart from that of the bishop make this function a normal aspect of their ministry by the close of the period.[11] However, in clear contrast to the official and civic character of the pagan priesthoods and the ceremonial, hereditary character of the Jewish priesthood, the ministry of Christian priests is conspicuously vocational, pastoral and didactic: the feeble efforts of the emperor Julian to encourage some social action by the pagan priesthoods of Antioch illustrate the practical difference well. The theology of order in the West after Gregory the Great lost the clarity of the Augustinian position in the complexities of controversy over the validity of irregular and simonaical ordinations, unresolved until the definitive work of Alexander of Hales secured the traditional position to be inherited by the principal scholastics. But the dignity of the priestly office as one which by divine election sets aside the one ordained as separated from the world for a vocation of great elevation and responsibility is one which although present from the beginning in the writers of the sub-apostolic age receives its most eloquent expression in the rhetoric of the patrician ascetics who transform the scope and potential of the episcopal office in the fourth century.

The medieval conception of the priesthood as oriented to liturgical function at the Eucharist served to obscure in the principal scholastic authors the proper distinction between the priesthood and the episcopate, but despite this the sacramental reference of the title to sacrifice is preserved. Thomas Aquinas is the principal systematic exponent of this conception when he says, *The Orders are directed to the sacrament of the Eucharist chiefly, and to the other sacraments consequently, for even the other sacraments flow from what is contained in that sacrament.*[12] He gives a terse definition of how this priestly power was instituted among the apostles: it is given, *as regards the principal act, before his passion at the supper when he said,* Take ye and eat, *wherefore he added,* Do this for a commemoration of me. *After the resurrection, however, he gave them the priestly power, as to its secondary act, which is to bind and loose.*[13] In commenting on a text wrongly attributed to S. John Chrysostom which appeared to suggest that the possession of

85

sanctity was enough to make a priest, Aquinas allows that in the (given) etymological sense of *sacerdos* as *sacer dans*, dispenser of holy things, this might be allowed, but in the prevailing usage of *sacerdos* the reference was always to the giving of sacred things by dispensing the sacraments.[14] This cultic orientation of the Christian ministry as sacerdotal because Eucharistic secures the fundamental character of ministerial priesthood as an order.

However, where Aquinas is less convincing is in the unhistorical attachment of each order to particular liturgical functions as exercised in the Roman rite of his time.[15] He does acknowledge that in more primitive times, on account of the fewness of minister, deacons undertook the various ministries undertaken by others, but this does not prevent him from attaching very specific theological value to a variety of contingent time-conditioned acts. Thus the priest is superior to the deacon because he handles the Eucharistic elements directly, whereas the deacon does so in a vessel, and the subdeacon handles the vessel alone. Because the priest is above all the celebrant of the Eucharist, and because participation in the Eucharist requires for its efficacy freedom from sin, the priest is therefore the proper minister of all the sacraments which have for their purpose the cleansing of sin: Baptism, penance and unction. This ceremonial-functionalist approach is particularly unfortunate in elucidating the teaching role of the principal orders: Aquinas states that *doctrine is a remote preparation for the reception of a sacrament; wherefore the announcement of doctrine is entrusted to the ministers.*[16] However, this responsibility for doctrine is then resolved into an ingenious and symbolic account of who reads what lesson at Mass, which blurs the distinction between the diaconate and the other orders and omits any conception of the teaching office beyond liturgical function.[17]

The influence of Aquinas' teaching on Order is evident in the late medieval tendency to resolve the exercise of cult into specifics of ceremonial observance. The process by which the primitive understanding of ordination as conferred by prayer and the laying on of hands was eclipsed by the identification of the matter of ordination with the conveyance of the liturgical objects pertaining to the order to be given demonstrates this ascendancy of the symbolic and strictly ritual interpretation of the ministerial office over the more fulsome patristic model. In particular the exiguous attachment of the teaching office to the exercise of holy order would have a deleterious effect on the conception of priestly ministry in the Church. This is most obvious both in the eclipse of any identifiably 'presbyteral' tasks assigned to the ordained priesthood in terms of presidency over the community or formation by instruction, and in the reduction of the episcopate to a jurisdictional eminence within the one order of priesthood, less distinct in fact than the difference supposed to obtain between a subdeacon and an acolyte. Jean Galot in his consideration of the theology of priesthood gives only cursory attention to the scholastic period, largely with reference to the superseded Western sevenfold enumeration of the ministerial orders.[18] The medieval understanding of priesthood despite its inadequacies deserves more attention, because in Aquinas and those who follow him the essential characteristics of ministerial priesthood are preserved: the sacramental character of ordination; its indelibility as a *signaculum*; and its specific reference to the Eucharist as the *locus* of the sacramental economy, for whose celebration the ministerial priesthood is constituted.

PRIESTHOOD AND CHARACTER

The issue of the indelibility of ordination, its sacramental character, is one which relates properly to the three-fold ministry of bishop, presbyter and deacon and not exclusively to the priesthood, but the principle of a charism that endows its recipient with a graced capacity which is subsequent to and not

87

included in those given at Baptism is of fundamental importance. In the New Testament the existence of such a charism
is derived from the admonition made to Timothy: *Do not neglect
the gift that is in you, which was given to you through prophecy with the
laying on of hands by the council of elders* (1 Tim. 4.14), a gift which
the apostle encourages him to employ in the preaching of the
gospel when he writes for this reason *I remind you to rekindle the
gift of God that is within you through the laying on of my hands* (2 Tim.
1.6). This giving of a spiritual gift by the performance of a
significatory act in ordination gives it its sacramental status,
and so elides the question of ordination given either outside
the communion of the Church or by and to the sinful with that
of the indelibility of Baptism in Augustine's comprehensive
treatment of the issue.[19] This treatment had its origin in the
particular circumstances of the Donatist schism, in which
rebaptism and reordination became the distinctive public
hallmarks of the controversy, and erected what had been a
particular characteristic *theologumen* of the African Church
under Tertullian and Cyprian into a systematic justification
for schism.

Augustine's treatment essentially separates validity
from fruitfulness in the administration of the sacraments:
the *signaculum* conferred by Baptism and ordination is an
endowment with the character of Christ proper to the
sacrament in question that is indelible (he compares it to a
soldier's tattoo[20]); the disposition of the recipient both in terms
of ecclesial communion and personal repentance is what
governs the fruitfulness which the sacramental grace given
achieves. What is the purpose of this character if it does not
of itself presume the operation of grace for salvation and the
right exercise of the state of life to which the recipient is called?
Augustine explains this with the principle of reviviscence:
*For it is one thing that Baptism should not be there, and another that it
should have no power to work salvation. For when men come to the peace
of the Catholic Church, then what was in them before they joined it, but*

did not profit them, begins at once to profit them.[21] In the particular
case of ordination he states: *the flaw lay in the separation from the
Church, which flaw is corrected by the peace of unity. There was no flaw
in the sacraments, which wherever they are, remain themselves.*[22] The
Augustinian doctrine of the sacramental seal, and the consequent validity of sacramental ministrations which take place
outside the communion of the Church, was confirmed in all
its essentials by the Council of Trent and remains the practice
of the Latin Church, albeit tempered in practice on the one
hand by a more sympathetic acknowledgement of the fruitful
working of grace among all believers, and on the other greater
rigour in judging the presence of the requisite matter and
form in the ordination rites of the Reformation communities.
The Tridentine decree follows the common teaching of the
medieval schools when it describes the sacramental character
as *an indelible mark, a spiritual mark, impressed upon the soul.*[23]

How is this character manifested specifically in the ministry
of priesthood? That Baptism confers a place in the priestly
people of God is apparent in connexion with the Eucharistic
offering in the *Dialogue* of Justin: *God testifies that all who through
this name offer the sacrifices which Jesus the Christ commanded, that is,
the Eucharist of the bread and the cup, which are offered in every part
of the world by Christians, are acceptable to him.*[24] S. Thomas in
considering the question of sacramental character expresses
the nature of the seal precisely in terms of the orientation
of the Christian towards beatitude and the exercise of cult
towards God: *the faithful are deputed to a two-fold end. First and
principally to the enjoyment of glory ... secondly ... to receive, or to
bestow on others, things pertaining to the worship of God.*[25] Because the
rite of the Christian religion is derived from Christ's priesthood,
the sacramental characters which conform us to Christ *are
nothing else but certain participations of Christ's priesthood, flowing from
Christ himself.*[26] This signification of the priesthood of Christ is
distinctive in allocating differences between Christians in the
exercise of ministry; configurative, in conforming the person

so marked with the appropriate orientation to cult; and dispositive, in consecrating the person to the appropriate personal holiness for the state entered. Richard Hooker carried the principle of indelibility into Anglican sacramental theology when despite his own reluctance to call ordination a sacrament in itself, he emphatically defends its indelible character: *They which once have received this power may not think to put it off and on like a cloak as the weather serveth ... once consecrated unto God they are made his peculiar inheritance for ever.*[27]

INDELIBLE CHARACTER IN CONTEMPORARY ECUMENICAL DIALOGUE

This common teaching has recently come into question as a consequence of the 2006 Cyprus Agreed Statement between Anglicans and Orthodox, which states: *bishops and presbyters do not possess an indelible mark as if ordination were a magic seal granting them personal power to celebrate the Eucharist or any other liturgical action, apart from the ecclesial body.*[28] This statement stands at some distance not only from the doctrine elucidated by Hooker but from the standard manuals of Orthodox theology which describe ordination as giving an ineluctable gift of grace to the soul of the recipient, and as unrepeatable according to the canons. Nor is it consistent: the Statement affirms that *the canonical data leave no doubt that, once the Church decided to depose a bishop or presbyter, they returned to the rank of layman ... and were in no way considered to retain their priesthood,* but then states *The fact that ministerial rehabilitation and restoration of such persons did not ... involve reordination, does not imply any recognition that they were bishops or priests during the period of such punishment.*[29] The Statement claims that *in the patristic tradition, priesthood is never understood as an office based on an objectified mark imprinted on the soul of the ordained person,* which *is in no way a ministry which involves division or classification within the ecclesial body.*[30] This conception of ministerial ordination as grounded not in a doctrine of character but in an ontology of relation has its origin in the ecclesiology of John Zizioulas, whose contribution to the Agreed Statement is significant here.

Zizioulas[31] considers that the Augustinian objectification of grace as a thing to be given and transmitted by virtue of a power possessed vitiates the idea of sacramental character by reducing the definition of ordination to something done to the individual recipient. He regards the evidence of the Greek patristic writers concerning ordination to be supportive of an ontology of relation: the bishop, priest or deacon receives his charism not because of an indelible seal but because he is made existentially an ambassador of the gospel in relation to others; because there is a supernatural *theosis* proper to ordination but related to the transfiguration of all creation; and because there is a typological substitution effected by ordination in which the priest or bishop in his presidency becomes an antitype for Christ in the Eucharistic community. The consequence of this is emphatically that if an ordained person is separated by discipline from the Eucharistic community in which his *ordo* is realised, he ceases to be ordained, although subsequent reconciliation is a recognition by the community of its past action in ordaining, not a concession to the indelibility of the seal.

However, it is difficult to recognise in this analysis either the canonical practice or the dogmatic tradition of the Orthodox Churches themselves: Zizioulas admits that a preponderance of Orthodox authorities acknowledge the indelible character of ordination, nor is it easy to reconcile his account of why reordination is not necessary to receive back into communion those who have 'ceased' to be clergy, when the evidence of those fathers such as S. Basil who mention reordination dwell on its sacrilegious character rather than its superfluity. Gregory of Nyssa describes ordination in terms as ontologically demanding as any in Augustine: *The same power of the word, again, also makes the priest venerable and honourable, separated, by the new blessing bestowed upon him, from his community with the mass of men. While but yesterday he was one of the mass, one of the people, he is suddenly rendered ... an instructor in hidden mysteries; and this he does without being at all changed in body or in form; but, while continuing to be in all appearance the man he was before, being, by some unseen power and grace, transformed in respect of his unseen soul to the higher condition.*[32] The language of the Agreed Statement insists to the contrary that there is no separation caused by ordination, and that the Church as the Eucharistic community has the right and responsibility to remove absolutely from the ministry those choose to relinquish their responsibilities or are deposed: *Any notion of 'indelible mark' would imply that the ordained individual possesses forever this peculiar mark of priesthood, which can never in any circumstances be removed or surrendered.*[33] But this is precisely what Hooker was able to say in explaining the continuity of the Church of England's polity on this point with the Augustinian doctrine: *suspensions may stop, and degradations may utterly cut off the use or exercise of power before given: but voluntarily it is not in the power of man to separate and pull asunder what God by his authority coupleth.*[34] Sacramental character is a particular participation in the priesthood of Jesus Christ which is perpetual, whether it be through the orientation towards beatitude given in the sacraments of initiation, or the particular cultic delegation which ordination conveys to constitute the Church as Eucharistic reality, an act which is indeed always relational but made objective by the permanent conformity of the individual to the mystery of Christ.

PRIESTHOOD AS A DELEGATION TO CULT

Christian priesthood has a three-fold character: the priesthood which belongs to the incarnate Christ himself; the priesthood which belongs to the people of God by virtue of their sacramental incorporation into him; the priesthood which in the celebration of the Eucharist perpetuates the commission made to the apostles that the sacrifice of Calvary might be continued in its effect by a sacramental sacrifice. The priesthood of Christ himself is merited by the perfect obedience of his incarnate life and exercised on Calvary in a way which is anticipated by the sacrificial system of the Temple, even if at its most funda-mental it is the indestructible life represented by the priesthood of Melchizedek that best exemplifies it. The priesthood which as a consequence of Christ's redemption belongs to the people of God is a priesthood which is corporate and which desig-nates the Church with a character of holiness. This endows all Christian moral living with a cultic orientation, as the good works which constitute authentic spiritual sacrifices are the 'liturgical' practices of the new royal priesthood built on Christ. The ministerial priesthood which is identified with the bishop or presbyter in his role as Eucharistic president and celebrant is a particular participation in the character of Christ as the priest who wills his sacrifice to be continued in a sacramental mode: as Jeremy Taylor writes, *in its proportion an instrument of applying the proper Sacrifice to all the purposes which it first designed.*[35]

Is it necessary that the person who presides over the Eucharistic celebration be one of the ministers who are mentioned in the New Testament exclusively in connection with other functions? John Zizioulas in his negative treatment of ministerial character stresses the importance placed on the role of the minister as an ambassador for Christ, the one who exercises *presbeia* on his behalf.[36] This ambassadorial role is not an external representation but a participation in the person of Christ himself, speaking in his name and with his authority. The one who performs this task as the Eucharistic president exercises this *presbeia* in an exemplary way, by effecting in the two-fold consecration of bread and wine the sacrament-sacrifice of the new covenant. The French cardinal and theologian of priesthood Pierre de Bérulle considered that through the insti-tution of the Eucharist Christ gave the character of his person to those whom he commissioned to continue the oblation: by

93

virtue of his incarnation he shares our nature; by virtue of his delegation at the Last Supper to the apostles, those who perpetuate their ministry through ordination act in Christ's person when they offer the Eucharist in his place with and for his Church. This participation in the personhood of Christ as ministerial priest, the particular character which pertains to ordained priesthood, is one which Bérulle does not hesitate to call a participation made particular by its imitation of the servanthood of Christ.[37] This is the necessary corrective to any sense of separation and autonomy which the character of ordination is meant to suggest, a Johannine commitment to a ministry of service which is always concomitant with the commission to offer the Eucharistic sacrifice.

Notes for Chapter 4

1 *ST*, III q 63 a 2.
2 A usage first found in Philo, see Barker, Margaret, *The Hidden Tradition of the Kingdom of God*, p 64.
3 Barker, *The Hidden Tradition of the Kingdom of God*, pp 72–2.
4 *ST*, III q 81 a 3.
5 Gore, Charles, *The Body of Christ*, p 312.
6 *ST*, III q 22 a 6.
7 See article *Ordre* in *Dictionnaire de Théologie Catholique*, 11.2.
8 Gregory of Nazianzus, *Ep* 171.
9 See Stone, Darwell, *A History of the Doctrine of the Holy Eucharist*, pp 46, 51.
10 See Stone, *History*, pp 47–8.
11 See Leo the Great, *Sermon* 48; Innocent I, *Letter to Decentius of Gubbio*.
12 *ST*, Suppl q 37 a 4.
13 *ST*, Suppl q 38 a 5.
14 *ST*, Suppl q 36 a 3.
15 *ST*, Suppl q 37 a 4.
16 *ST*, Suppl q 37 a 4.
17 *ST*, Suppl q 37 a 4, 5.
18 Galot, Jean, *The Theology of Priesthood*, pp 177–8.
19 See Leeming, Bernard, *Sacramental Theology*, pp 152–61; 455–61.
20 See Leeming, *Sacramental Theology*, p 152.
21 Augustine, *De Baptismo*, 6. 9 13, 14.
22 Augustine, *Contra Epistulam Parmeniani*, 2. 13, 28.
23 Council of Trent, Session 7 Canon 9 on the sacraments in general in Tanner & Alberigo, *Decrees*, vol 2 p 685.
24 Justin Martyr, *Dialogue with Trypho*, c 116.
25 *ST*, III q 63 a 3.
26 *ST*, III q 63 a 3.
27 Hooker, *Ecclesiastical Polity*, V 77 (3).

28 *The Church of the Triune God*, VI 22.
29 *The Church of the Triune God*, VI 23.
30 *The Church of the Triune God*, VI 25.
31 Zizioulas, John, *Being as Communion*, pp 225–36.
32 Gregory of Nyssa, *Homily on the Baptism of Christ*, in Library of Nicene and Post-Nicene Fathers, second series vol 5 p 519.
33 *The Church of the Triune God*, VI 22.
34 Hooker, *Ecclesiastical Polity*, V 77 (3).
35 See More and Cross, *Anglicanism*, p 495.
36 Zizioulas, *Being as Communion*, pp 220, 227.
37 See Michel, Dupuy, *Bérulle et le Sacerdoce*, pp 131–4.

5

Rite

What does the Mass look like? ... a reading party followed by a shared meal.[1]

Nicholas Lash

THE RITUAL CHARACTER OF CHRISTIAN CULT

The Christian cult conforms to the sacramental economy
by being attentive to the outward and visible signs of its
celebration, because it is the archetypal exercise of the virtue of
religion by the fundamental sacramental sign which is Christ's
mystical body. The Temple cult is superseded by the sacrifice
of Christ it anticipates, and the New Testament contains no
new ceremonial system to regulate the practice of worship
for the royal priesthood which succeeds it. Indeed, Paul's use
of the term *liturgist* would appear to spiritualise the function
of cult and resolve its meaning to that inward consecration
of intention which makes all good works a *sacrifice of praise*.
However, the conviction as old as Ignatius of Antioch that the
Church has an altar and a sacrifice and a visible ministerial
hierarchy with responsibility for them comes to have architectural, artistic and ceremonial consequences. Persecution and
poverty impede without extinguishing the expression of this
principle in the first three centuries of the Church's life; the
Constantinian peace brings with it a new expansiveness that

97

the consecration of the great basilica at Tyre, described in Eusebius, illustrates,[2] and the public sacralisation of Christian liturgical practice, places and vessels. Around this sacred space emerges a rich anagogical perception of liturgical practice, in which the action of the Eucharist becomes invested with signs of secular reverence transposed into worship, and the sacral character of the rite anticipates on earth of the worship in heaven of the Apocalypse. Liturgy expresses the anticipation of beatitude by the celebration of a sacramental sacrifice: the celebration of the sacrifice constitutes and enrols the people of God as holy and consecrated themselves, and so gives them a fundamental moral orientation towards the risen Christ.

Iconoclasm in both East and West is the enemy of this theological principle: a rejection of the sacramental economy except in the most circumscribed sense and a protest against the doctrine of analogy in worship, that any human representation of cult could anticipate or evoke the worship which will be the life of the blessed in heaven. The experience of iconoclasm in the East secured once and for all the analogical principle in the liturgical practice of the Church, to such an extent that in the cultural circumstances which have constrained the Orthodox Churches the liturgy has come to contain and sustain the entire practice and transmission of the Christian faith. In the Latin West the situation has been more complex. Iconoclasm has been accompanied by a much more conflicted sense of what constitutes the sacred in art, and the pressure of theological controversy especially concerning the sacrificial character of the Eucharist ossified certain practices and rites which in the usual course of organic development would have adapted more freely to changed circumstances.

DEDICATION AND THE ANAGOGICAL CHARACTER OF CULT

The teaching of Thomas Aquinas about the way in which Christian liturgical worship consecrates places and objects to be sacred begins with considering why there should be such places and objects when the sacrifice which is being represented sacramentally in the Eucharist took place outside and the Last Supper which institutes the sacrament itself in an ordinary supper-room. In response to this Aquinas makes the fundamental analogy between the Church as the household of faith and the dedication of particular buildings to be representative of that household in the offering of Christian worship. Because the building in which the celebration of the Eucharist takes place denotes the Church, it therefore takes its name, and is consecrated as such *to represent the holiness which the Church acquired from the Passion, as well as to denote the holiness of them who have to receive this sacrament.*[3] Aquinas locates particular significance in the consecration of the altar, which signifies Christ himself and his holiness. His argument here blends some contemporary legislation about the aptness of celebrating outside a consecrated building with the fundamental principle of designating places as sacred; however, the anagogical relation remains the concrete justification of his argument, the symbolic significance of the building and its sacred furniture corresponding sacramentally to the spiritual reality of the Church as Christ's body and Christ as the head of the Church.[4]

The consecration which these buildings and objects receive is not an infusion of grace: no inanimate thing can be capable of this, but they can be given what Aquinas calls *special spiritual virtue from the consecration, whereby they are rendered fit for divine worship, so that man derives devotion from them, making him more fitting for divine functions.*[5] This sacred character has a particular connection with the cultic holiness, the designation as holy by imputation, which belongs to the *ecclesia* from which the building derives its name: sin dissipates this, which is why both desecration by bloodshed and heretical consecration require the repetition of the orthodox rite, in contrast to the ministration of the sacraments properly so called by the unworthy and those outside the communion of the Church, which are indelible. This theology of Dedication is particularly significant in Laurence Hemming's account of contemporary liturgical malaise.[6] Just as the cult of the temple in Jerusalem with its sanctuary and veil and hierarchy operated as a microcosm of the creation, in which the expiation made by the high priest served not simply to avoid the punishment for sin but to reconstitute human participation in the integrity of the divine purpose for the whole cosmos, so the dedication of churches, far from being simply a pragmatic or legal matter, is a sacramental means by which the archetypal Christian appropriation of the dedication theme in keeping the octave of Easter is made local to each place in which the atoning sacrifice is now offered. Hemming is particularly critical here of the suppression of the actual liturgical octave of the Dedication which the simplifications of the 1950s brought about in the Roman rite, which he sees as a rich reference to the Temple obscured.

Aquinas is largely unhistorical in the critical attention he brings to the evidence for liturgical practices and habits (as his implausible argument about glass chalices testifies). Richard Hooker by contrast has to justify his notion of the sacred in material things after a period of intense iconoclasm in England, and in the face of continuing resistance to any sense of consecration and dedication to religious purposes, established in a forceful and persuasive puritan ideology. He begins his argument with an account of how the exercise of religion in a particular place began with Adam in Eden and continued to the establishment of the Temple in Jerusalem, which even when restored after the exile was still *the wonder of the whole world*. The Church at first worshipped of necessity in private, and then in time of persecution in secret, until the conversion of the emperors meant that *that which the Church before either could not or durst not do, was with all alacrity performed*.[7] These buildings Hooker explicitly calls temples: *no cost was spared, nothing judged too dear which that way should be spent*.[8] Hooker justifies first the dedication of such places by public ceremonies, which at once serve to dedicate them as assemblies not of private congregations but of the whole Church duly constituted for worship, and (and here Hooker is typically English in his anxiety about the legal title to property) *to make God himself their owner.*[9] The religious solemnity of the rite of dedication is a notification of the holiness of what will take place within.

Furthermore, Hooker justifies the dedication of churches to saints and angels in their titles, which (although for him this has no suggestion of patronage) is useful in recalling their virtues and their sacrifices.[10] The partitioning of the church into a chancel for the clergy and a nave for the people, in which both orders are divided according to dignity, is attacked by Hooker's opponents as an explicit revival of the Jewish Temple, which he justifies partly by denying there is any place of sacrifice according to his own view of Eucharist and priesthood, and partly by appealing to the architectural arrangements of the Temple as apt and appropriate.[11] His theology of the sanctuary lacks an altar, the insertion of which into the ecclesial built environment by the Laudians was to provoke the subsequent controversies of the 1630s and contribute to the end of the comprehensive national Church in England.[12] But even if Hooker denies a place of sacrifice in the Church, he embraces the appropriateness of splendour even at a time of conspicuous neglect. Again the Jewish cult is invoked as a precedent: the tabernacle in the desert was *beautiful, gorgeous and rich*, and the temple *a spectacle of admiration to the whole world*; the which *curious exornations* have both a mystical role in anticipating Christ but also a natural one as an offering to God and a testimony to his majesty.[13] He concludes his argument with an appeal to the appropriate edification of the building according to its end: *Churches receive as everything else their chief perfection from the end whereunto they serve. Which end being the public worship of God, they are in this consideration houses of greater dignity than any provided for meaner purposes.*[14]

Hooker's argument here reflects Thomas Aquinas' diversion of the Aristotelian virtue of magnificence to pious ends; it does not embrace the Thomist particularism about the special virtue which consecration imparts to individual objects, and which finds its most expansive analysis in the liturgical commentaries of his contemporary Durandus of Mende. Durandus is not an uncritical proponent of ecclesiastical pomp: he famously states in the middle of a lengthy description of the ornaments of the Church that before Pope Zephyrinus the chalices were of wood and the priests of gold, whereas in his own time the opposite is true.[15] But his appeal to the mystical sense of liturgical interpretation is justified by referring to the exegesis of Scripture: just as the reader finds there matter which requires historical, allegorical, tropological and anagogical consideration, so the rites of the Church require attention to their significance in the same modes. David Berger has argued that Thomas Aquinas was making a deliberate and considered decision to adopt the Durandine model of liturgical exegesis at a time when the exaggeration of some symbolists and the bad odour into which the Berengarian Eucharistic controversy had led such interpretations was threatening the integrity of the entire method in the face of a more rationalist and positivist approach. He contends that far from being outmoded or reduced to the status of *useless repetitions*, the anagogical recapitulation of the liturgical texts and rubrics of the historic Latin rite actually *at all times recall in their concrete representation a mystery in the life of Jesus that has its centre in the paschal mystery*.[16]

ANAGOGY AND ETHICISM

Catherine Pickstock has located the contemporary liturgical malaise and the failure of the high hopes for liturgical reform which followed the Second Vatican Council precisely in this failure to recognise what she calls *liturgical stammer and constant re-beginning*, in favour of a rationalist assumption that the primitive can be revivified by anachronistic enlightenment conceptions of simplicity, pragmatism, ethicism and linearity.[17] For her, a true liturgical reform, necessary in the context of a rite fossilised by the sort of baroque Cartesianism which repelled the young Joseph Ratzinger, would not be 'a reading party followed by a meal', but a rite which resolutely refused inculturation into modernity's habits of thought and speech. Nicholas Lash does not claim in his lapidary description of what the Mass should look like that this necessarily privileges simplicity over complexity or primitivism over the insight of the Christian centuries. But he does insist on the *legibility* of the *res sacramenti*: the more the rite emphasises its meal-like character, the more evident it will be that Christ is truly present in the Eucharistic elements, the Scriptures read and the assembly gathered, and the more apparent the sacrificial character of that meal will be. The hiddeness of Christ in the Eucharist, whether it be the *latens deitas* of Aquinas, the veiled God of Alphonsus de Liguori or the pyx-dwelling prisoner of Father Faber, is for Lash an aberrant devotional current which received unfortunate dogmatic sanction by the decision of the Council of Trent to separate its consideration of the Eucharistic presence from that of the sacrifice of the Mass.[18]

This significatory priority in the presentation of the Eucharist would seem also to find support in the exegesis of sacrifice given by Anscar Vonier. He emphasises that the sacrifice is contained entirely in the external signification given: *it contains no more than it signifies; for if it did it would not be a sacrament, it would be an absolute act of God's omnipotence.*[19] He is prepared to justify subsequent *significations and symbolisms, which are like so many ramifications and radiations of the divine sign,*[20] but the essential signification remains neither more nor less than the absolute appropriateness of the bread and the wine for their sacramental task. However, although Vonier is so emphatic about the ritual and sacramental character of the sacrifice in the Eucharist, he couples this with an equally strong doctrine of concomitance, whereby the *island of solid rock* which this sacramental sacrifice comprises is surrounded by *a sea of wonderful mystery … the vitalities of Christ's infinite Personality.*[21] This concomitant presence is indeed an act of divine omnipotence, because it is a productive act of God Himself; but it does not constitute what is present in the Eucharist by virtue of its being the principal sacrament of the new covenant. The reality of this presence of Christ in his fullness, Vonier's *sea of wonderful mystery*, gives rise to the *cultus* of the blessed sacrament as such within the Eucharistic rite, in both the allegorical ascriptions of Durandus and such practices as exposition, benediction and Eucharistic processions. The *laetus deus* of S. Thomas is the Christ whose Passion is renewed sacramentally by the consecration of bread and wine, but whose sacrifice under those signs of separation is one whose value is not made the less by being offered by the priest whose now glorified humanity is inseparably and hypostatically united to the Word.

Vonier says of those who find the fact of sacramental consecration inadequate to explain the immolation in the Eucharist and instead ascribe it to *a sort of abasement or humiliation compared with his natural state of glory* that *such an explanation of the Eucharistic sacrifice comes not from the centre of the sacramental doctrine, but has been brought in from quite another realm of Christian thought; it has been borrowed from the sphere of ethics.*[22] Here he is speaking principally to criticise the destruction theories of Eucharistic sacrifice which predominated in the Latin Church after the Council of Trent, but the appeal to the ethical remains contentious because of the way in which liturgical reform has appeared to privilege the moral experience of the celebrating community at the expense of objective adoration in contemporary practice. David Berger writes that the Thomist understanding of the liturgy takes its fundamental orientation not from pedagogic or indeed pastoral circumstances but from the law of worship: the sacrament of the Eucharist is ordained first for the worship of God, acceptable because it is the sacrifice of Christ whose sinless priesthood makes him the perfect adorer; and second for the sanctification of humankind, which thereby is made ready for beatitude. This sanctification is achieved by the instrumental causality of Christ's humanity which acts as an organ for his divine nature and makes the operation of sacramental grace physical and not moral. This has fundamental significance for the way in which the Eucharistic rite is celebrated. If sacramental grace is given *ex opere operato*, but only in a moral or psychological sense, then the celebration of the Eucharist will be above all attentive to the practical circumstances of its active participants, and subject to all the enthusiasms and restraints of secular pedagogy.

The consequence of this for Roman Catholic liturgical reform has been according to the Dominican theologian Aidan Nichols, *a utilitarian or pragmatist philosophical infrastructure for which happiness or usefulness is the key to truth ... a predominance of ethical values over strictly religious ones.*[23] Similarly in the Church of England, anxiety about the unfavourable or complicated impression traditional liturgical forms might provoke has licensed virtually complete abdication of the use of such forms if the context can be labelled (by the established hierarchy, of course) a 'Fresh Expression'. This ethical sacramentalism is Scotist in character and as such has been portrayed by Catherine Pickstock (among others) as an integral part of the incursion of the secular into the liturgical world, a self-inflicted retreat of the sacred and a substitution of self-improvement by the community for the more authentic liturgical 'enrolment' by which the celebration of the Mass actually constitutes the Church. This eclipse of Christian order in liturgical celebration substitutes active participation for sacramental character, and the cultivation of community-tutored ethical improvement for the sacral microcosm of acceptable worship which each Eucharistic celebration with its explicitly cosmic reference evokes.

Christian rite must take its inspiration from the instrumental effectiveness of Christ's human nature in the Eucharistic rite, both as perfect adorer of the Father and as the victim who nourishes the priestly people with himself, if it is to avoid solipsistic activism and a merely moral aspiration to benefit from its celebration. This follows from the way in which our redemption is accomplished: the objective work of salvation is accomplished by God through the incarnation, a tangible taking of human nature which thus becomes the instrument of all grace given to save; our subjective salvation likewise relies for the bestowal of grace on the tangible sacramental signs which God as principal agent uses, in a way which bestows spiritually the grace signified by the proper action of each appointed sign. If a conception of liturgical practice which sees the community gathered to celebrate as the objective norm is substituted for this latreutic orientation, then the constitution of the assembly as elected to beatitude and initiated into this election by sacramental character is lost, and replaced by an activism which celebrates what is simply morally efficacious and which depends for its effectiveness on the pedagogic and pastoral quality of what is done. Lawrence Hemming notes this as a rare failure of Catherine Pickstock to unmask secularisation in the liturgy, when she describes the liturgical community as visible and the work done by it as mysterious, whereas he emphasises that the sacramental work which is visible constitutes the *ecclesia*, which is the mystical (because invisible) manifestation of the body which the sacrament produces. He quotes De Lubac to support this: *he himself is the body whose food those who eat it become.*[24]

THE REFORM OF THE CONTEMPORARY WESTERN RITE

Anxiety about the character of liturgical reform in the West and the need to revisit many of its premises and assumptions in the light of contemporary malaise and secularisation received new vigour and impetus when Joseph Ratzinger was elected Pope as Benedict XVI in 2005. His experience of the liturgy prior to the Second Vatican Council made him grateful for the piety of his youth but impatient at the rubricism and ossification of the rite of Mass as actually experienced in the great majority of Roman Catholic Churches untouched by the principles of the pre-conciliar Liturgical Movement. However, immediately after the close of the Council, the drastic character of the reform as actually carried out, in which the Roman rite as it had been known in language, calendar and ceremonial was effectively abolished and replaced by a synthetic, participatory and demotic celebration, and the toleration of even more innovative styles of worship among experimental groups, led him to reconsider the success of the reform and its consonance with the intentions of the Council Fathers in their decree on the Sacred Liturgy, *Sacrosanctum Consilium*. That his most systematic treatment of the liturgical question borrows its title, *The Spirit of the Liturgy*, from the seminal work of Romano Guardini on liturgical renewal demonstrates that Ratzinger does not write out of an integrist position, and that although he has sympathy with those whom he describes as treated like lepers for their attachment to the Tridentine liturgy, he does not share their refusal of the new. However, he is powerfully critical of the mentality and method which carried out the reform of the Roman rite as it took place, and in his policy as Pope has encouraged both a heightened sense of the sacred in celebrations using the reformed texts, and allowed free use of the old as a means of encouraging a fruitful reform of the reform.

Ratzinger's liturgical theology predates the ideological assault on rationalist secularism which characterises the liturgical critique of the Radical Orthodoxy movement, and does not go as far as to locate the source of contemporary malaise in the crisis of late scholasticism. Indeed, Ratzinger compares the

Roman rite to a fresco: whitewashed over until the Liturgical Movement of the twentieth century revealed it momentarily in a way which was canonised by the Second Vatican Council, and then obscured again by its exposure to a corrosive contemporary atmosphere.[25] His relative lack of interest in scholastic theology means that his consideration of liturgical questions feels more serene about the recent past than does that of many more recent commentators who take their inspiration from his critical stance but who are more obviously motivated by Henri de Lubac's reintegration of the supernatural into a renewed Thomism. Moreover, his interests are principally expressed in practical terms: how a church should be ordered, the sort of music that should accompany the liturgy, and what the celebration of the Church's year should contribute to the sanctification of time. This is a pastoral theology, not because it subordinates what has been received from the past to contemporary preferences, but because it looks to establish the faith of the people of God more securely from the liturgy, which the Second Vatican Council described as the source and summit of Christian life.

Ratzinger begins by placing liturgy as the expression of the cult which orders human living towards beatitude: *Ultimately, it embraces the ordering of the whole of human life ... Man becomes glory for God, puts God, so to speak, into the light (and that is what worship is), when he lives towards God.*[26] Ethical living without worship is impossible because: *Worship, that is, the right kind of cult, of relationship with God, is essential for the right kind of human existence in the world ... it lays hold in advance of a more perfect life, and in so doing, gives our present life its proper measure.*[27] This worship is necessarily instituted by God, not devised by us: the worship of the golden calf is an image and warning of the human instinct to replace the demands of authentic worship with the circularity of self-appointed cult. Moreover, authentic Christian worship is not a transposition of synagogue worship into new circumstances, it is Temple worship, possessing both sacrifice and priesthood, defined by the risen Christ: *We do indeed participate in the heavenly liturgy, but this participation is mediated to us through earthly signs, which the Redeemer has shown to us as the place where his reality is to be found.*[28] This dispensation means that time is marked in a sacred way through the weekly recurrence of the Lord's Day which is at once theophany and Sabbath, and through the celebration of the cycle of feasts which evoke the mysteries of Christ, Mary and the saints; that space is given an orientation by the expectant offering of the Eucharist by priest and people turning together towards the Lord; that sacred art which takes its inspiration from the liturgy and which serves it as a manifestation of divine life in its subjects is not the same as art with a religious theme; that liturgical music has as its inspiration the service of the Word, not that of the *ethos*.

These principles of worship are mediated through rite, which is in the lapidary definition of the pagan Festus adopted by Ratzinger *approved practice in the administration of sacrifice.*[29] The rites of the Church, although they are appropriate to the particular cultures in which they first flourished, are capable of adaptation and transposition in ways which do not require and in fact exclude violent revision, as they have an organic, rather than a mechanistic character. Ratzinger is therefore critical of the way in which this sense of the liturgy as a patrimonial possession of the Church to be preserved was lost in the wake of the Second Vatican Council, when the Church for a time forgot her own mandate to be at the service of Sacred Tradition and instead used her authority to manufacture.[30] However, he does not envisage simply re-instating the former practice, and in particular he has little to say about the exclusive use of the Latin language which was so formidable a barrier to active participation in the Roman rite as it was known until 1964. Instead he reflects on the value of neglected or derided practices whose restoration would be a tangible resacralisation: the repeated sign of the Cross, prayer towards the East, kneeling, liturgical silence and the dignified vesture of altar and clergy.

The preference for solutions drawn from Augustine rather than Thomas that characterises Ratzinger's theological method grounds this project of resacralisation in the transcendental property of beauty. Thomas Aquinas only arguably distinguishes beauty from the good as a whole; it is the Augustinian tradition re-pristinated in scholastic terms by Bonaventure and in contemporary theological thought by Hans Urs von Balthasar which grounds the aspiration for sacrality on a firmer footing than aestheticism. The modern suspicion of beauty, especially beauty associated with ornament, in architecture, music and art intended for worship represents a Kantian intrusion into the Augustinian ethical sphere which has always sought to relate the beautiful to the One who is its source: *O beauty, so ancient and so new.* This principle of beauty as a transcendental quality which of itself makes language and symbol catechetical in the celebration of the liturgy suffers from a contemporary decadence which reflects the broader dissociation of sensibility in Western culture since the Reformation. There has been since then an instability in the Western liturgical ethos in terms of sacred art which has made the Roman rite particularly susceptible to 'whitewash' that overlays its integrity with secular and merely aesthetic idioms. The romantic revival of the nineteenth century supplanted the unselfconscious expansiveness of the baroque with the archaeological particularity of the gothic revival, taking its scholarship from the Benedictine reformation at Solesmes and its whiff of absinthe-and-occultism from the novels of Huysmans. Nor was the Eastern rite exempt from this instability of ethos by virtue of some timeless integrity of its own: the neo-classical Churches with their naturalistic icons and operatic deacons which typify Russian practice during this period demonstrate the same problem.

It is unsurprising then that when the principles of the Liturgical Movement came to be canonised by the Second Vatican Council, the ensuing revision of the rites themselves took place in a context which succumbed entirely to the contemporary aesthetic of modernism which was functionalist and unsympathetic to the vital role of the symbolic in liturgical practice. The Mass was to be made participatory, communitarian and demotic: a liturgy without elitism in language and ceremonial for the unchurched factory worker; a liturgy which emphasised the pedagogic for the Christian deprived of any other catechesis under communism; a liturgy purged of the distinctively European exigencies of Greco-Roman culture for the newly liberated colonial peoples. The social and political changes which have, since the reform, radically altered the context for which it was intended, have meant that liturgical revision now needs to take place at an almost constant rate to keep pace with the original aspiration of popular inclusion, while the pedagogic fruits which were rightly such an important motivation have been dissipated by the complete failure of the artistic style which went with them to convey the transcendent effectively. The Dominican Aidan Nichols emphasises this in his own liturgical theology when he says: *The Modernist understanding of architectural language simply cannot be combined with the Catholic tradition's own approach to Church construction.*[31]

LITURGICAL ORIENTATION

A particular *locus* of this dissatisfaction with the received assumptions of contemporary practice is liturgical orientation and the place of the altar in Christian cult. The symbolic significance of the altar as especially representative of Christ remains consistently expressed in the contemporary liturgical form for its consecration, inheriting both the anagogical exegesis of Durandus and the theology of consecration formulated by Aquinas. However, in practice the recent and unmandated insistence on the celebrant at Mass facing the people in the nave across the altar has resulted either in the widespread destruction of altars which although integral to the design and purpose of their churches happen not to be adaptable to such celebrations, or to the introduction of often flimsy and inadequate substitute altars which sit unhappily in front of their neglected predecessors. Even if the motivation behind this change were sound, the apparent willingness to discard what was universally considered to be the most sacred of the Church's consecrated objects has been inimical to the sense of the holy which the Tradition proposes. However, it is evident that much of the historical scholarship upon which this change was based is insubstantial or dependent on the apparent evidence of unusual and specialist buildings such as the Roman basilicas of the martyrs.[32] In fact, the principal aim of this innovation has been to promote precisely that ethical cultivation of community celebration which is destructive of genuine liturgical life, and which occludes by its very circularity and introspection the orientation to beatitude which sacrifice and communion establish.

The turning of both priest and people together towards the East, far from being a cultic exclusion by the celebrant of the active participation of the laity, is rather an act of fundamental cultic solidarity, in which the mystical body of the Lord is realised through an offering which is actually orientated towards the transcendent. Instead of this consistent Christian practice which unites all past generations in a solidarity of expectant prayer, what Origen described as *an act which symbolises the soul looking to where the true light rises*,[33] contemporary Western Christians are all too often constrained to worship in liturgical spaces which are both badly adapted practically and conceived in an entirely unhistoric sense as being authentic because meal-like. This difficulty is made worse by the detachment of the Cross from the liturgical furniture of the altar, so that instead of being united in a common turning towards the sign of Christ's redemptive act which stands over the place where he renews that sacrifice in sacramental form, the people experience the celebrant as the one who facilitates the work of the assembly, and whose subjective manner and presence set its tone far more obviously than the iconic force of the crucifix. This iconoclastic combination of an eclectic antiquarianism and a rationalist exclusion of the transcendental from worship has done immense physical and moral damage to the environment of the Christian cult. The contemporary standard of liturgical celebration, at least until the pontificate of Benedict XVI brought the critique of this standard into the mainstream of theological and liturgical discourse, seems designed to produce what Aidan Nichols calls *convivial puritans*:[34] Christians who locate communion in the activity of the community.

The Anglican experience of liturgical reform is salutary and significant here. The English Reformation was thoroughly iconoclastic and directed its attention particularly at the images of the saints and all that pertained to the Eucharist as sacrifice. Although Hooker is an advocate of moderation in the face of the contemporary puritan pressure to complete reform on a Calvinistic model, he shares their rejection of priest, altar and sacrifice in the Christian cult. However, the revival of these terms and things which took place in the so-called Arminian reaction under Charles I became emphatically focused on the restoration of altars, rested and railed in a permanent place in each parish chancel. The variety of practice which had obtained in the period from Elizabeth's accession to the death of James I began to give way to the restoration of the communion table altar-wise as the Anglican norm, and indeed so unpopular was this change that it became a significant contributory factor to the failure of the Anglican establishment to maintain itself as the accepted national Church.

When the followers of the Oxford Movement began to interest themselves in what they called ecclesiology, the principle of a communion table set altar-wise was therefore in possession, even if polemical considerations meant it necessary to emphasise its use as a writing desk or repository for clothes in contrast to the reverent gloom of the gothic ideal. Their innovation was to emphasise the importance of the priest's position at the altar: rather than adopt the rubrical peculiarity of standing at the north end of the altar as *The Book of Common Prayer* seemed to require, they made a party point of the eastward position, a sacrificial stance which placed the priest in a mediatorial position of leadership, complemented by the wearing of vestments, lighting of candles and even the burning of incense. Joseph Ratzinger has drawn particular attention to this aspect of the Catholic Revival in the Church of England, an example of what he has called the *Catholic potential* which characterises its periodic reassertion of continuity with the pre-Reformation Church in more than a simply generic sense.[35] What the Oxford Movement understood virtually from the start was that the doctrinal positions which were being extracted from the Anglican formularies and historic divinity would need to be taught and expressed in the conduct of public worship. Even if the immediate founding fathers of the Movement went slowly in these things to begin with, the transformation of the Gothic Revival from a world of whimsical paste tournaments and fake hermits to a comprehensive artistic expression of Christian doctrine and practice was carried out by their disciples with learning, skill and application, all the more remarkable given the prevailing utilitarian culture in which they were reared.

THE RESTORATION OF AUTHENTIC CHRISTIAN CULT

Christian liturgical rite, approved practice in the offering of sacrifice, creates a rich sacred landscape of text, symbol and ceremony through which the human senses are prepared through a sacramental asceticism to apprehend beatitude. The organic integrity of these rites arises from the response of culture to revelation and evolves according to the attentive fidelity of each generation to the sacramental economy by which the Lord constitutes the Church as his Body. Positivistic incursion into this inherently traditional process is inevitably iconoclastic because the resonance of tradition cannot be encapsulated in bureaucratic-legalist structures. This is as true of rubrical and textual ossification as it is of the substitution of the manufactured for the organic. The Augustinian principle of intelligibility in the sacramental economy ought to serve as a preservative against both the reduction of cult to incantation and the detachment of cult from tradition. Contemporary liturgical practice suffers from the consequences of both these distortions: because the Reformation controversies and the possibilities of printing made enforced uniformity an achievable aspiration, the liturgical rites of the West became unnaturally immutable, and so victims of their own immobility at a time when a corresponding crisis of transcendence in both theology and art inevitably made their fabricated replacements emerge from a hermeneutic of rupture.

The reconstitution of a liturgical order able to draw fruitfully on its perennial resources will not be easy; nor is it in any way fulfilled by the sort of bland eclecticism which characterises the confected Eucharistic prayers of the current Church of England prayer book *Common Worship*. The liturgical theology of Joseph Ratzinger is astute in recognising that coercive impositions of uniformity produce an economy only as stable as the regime which requires them, and that the fabrication of liturgical texts and rites by ecclesiastical bureaucracies inevitably reproduces all the historical, theological, artistic and social limitations of knowledge and perspective which 'experts' perpetuate wherever they work. His policy as Pope has reflected this, in abandoning the positivist obsession with uniformity and encouraging the reviviscence of the Liturgical Movement through the parallel use of both forms of the Roman Rite. Here the example of the Oxford Movement has been important. His theology is perhaps less engaged with the consequences of the crisis of the supernatural which contemporary critics have placed at the heart of the internal dissolution of liturgical living, and which gives rise to the pietistic, ethical and utilitarian preferences of contemporary rites. The authentic and integral celebration of the Christian rite, because it enacts the sacrifice which constitutes the mystical body, orders all human living as liturgical: liturgical in offering Christ as the only acceptable worship to the Father; liturgical in the definitive ordered enrolment which sacramental character bestows; liturgical in anticipating the beatific vision for which sacramental grace is given.

Notes for Chapter 5

1 Lash, Nicholas, *Theology for Pilgrims*, p 203.
2 Eusebius of Caesarea, *History of the Church*, 10, 3–4.
3 *ST*, III q 83 a 3.
4 *ST*, III q 83 a 3.
5 *ST*, III q 83 a 3.
6 Hemming, Lawrence, *Liturgy as a Revelation*, pp 1–9.
7 Hooker, Richard, *Ecclesiastical Polity*, V 11 (2).
8 Hooker, *Ecclesiastical Polity*, V 11 (3).
9 Hooker, *Ecclesiastical Polity*, V 12 (3).
10 Hooker, *Ecclesiastical Polity*, V 13 (1).
11 Hooker, Ecclesiastical Polity, V 14.
12 See Fincham, Kenneth & Tyacke, Nicholas, *Altars Restored: The Changing Face of English Religious Worship, 1547–c1700*.
13 Hooker, *Ecclesiastical Polity*, V 15 (4).
14 Hooker, *Ecclesiastical Polity*, V 16 (1).
15 Durandus of Mende, *Rationale Divinorum*, 3.4.
16 Berger, David, *Thomas Aquinas and the Liturgy*, p 37.
17 Pickstock, Catherine, *After Writing*, pp 170–6; 192–8.
18 Lash, *Theology for Pilgrims*, pp 198–200.
19 Vonier, Anscar, *Key*, p 67.
20 Vonier, *Key*, p 70.
21 Vonier, *Key*, p 144.
22 Vonier, *Key*, p 37.
23 Nichols, Aidan, *Looking at the Liturgy. A Critical View of its Contemporary form*, p 21.
24 Hemming, *Worship as a Revelation*, pp 77–80.
25 Ratzinger, Joseph, *The Spirit of the Liturgy*, pp 7–8.
26 Ratzinger, *The Spirit of the Liturgy*, p 20.
27 Ratzinger, *The Spirit of the Liturgy*, p 21.
28 Ratzinger, *The Spirit of the Liturgy*, p 61.

29 Ratzinger, *The Spirit of the Liturgy*, p 159.
30 Ratzinger, Joseph, *God and the World. Believing and Living in our time. A conversation with Peter Seewald*, pp 414–16.
31 Nichols, *Looking at the Liturgy*, p 89.
32 See Lang, Uwe, *Turning towards the Lord: Orientation in Liturgical Prayer.*
33 Origen, *Prayer*, 32.
34 Nichols, *Looking at the Liturgy*, p 69.
35 See his Foreword to Lang, *Turning Towards the Lord*, p 12.

6

Cure

Who but an atheist could think of leaving the world without having first made up his account? Without confessing his sins, and receiving that absolution which he knew he had one in the house authorised to give him? He … will lament the want of that absolution without which no sinner can be safe.[1]

Henry Fielding

THE FORGIVENESS OF SIN IN THE CHURCH

Thomas Aquinas describes the function of the Christian ministerial priesthood as two-fold: first, the offering of sacrifice; and second, the forgiveness of sin.[2] The act of atonement is made by the expiatory sacrifice which is offered, and is then applied to those who need its benefit in a way which raises their repentance to be a sacramental act. This sacramental act is founded on the preaching of repentance announced by John the Baptist as the sign of the nearness of the Kingdom of God, and fulfilled by Christ himself whose declaration of the forgiveness of sins is both a demonstration of his divine power and the cause of his condemnation. His disciples are called to preach repentance and the forgiveness of sins (Lk. 24.47) and this is reflected in the prototypical example of apostolic preaching by Peter given in Acts 2: *Repent, and be baptised every one of you in the name of Jesus Christ, so that your sins may be forgiven; and you will receive the gift of the Holy Spirit.*

119

It is Baptism which figures as the principal sacramental sign of repentance in this preaching, and the difficulty of forgiving post-baptismal sin is emphasised by the warning given in the letter to the Hebrews: *For it is impossible to restore again to repentance those who have once been enlightened ... since on their own they are crucifying again the Son of God and are holding him up to contempt* (Heb. 6.4–6). However, elsewhere in the New Testament there is evidence that the problem of post-baptismal sin was being considered in a way which allowed for some adjudication by the community, both as a matter of principle and in individual cases. The first letter of John introduces the distinction between sin which is deadly and sin which is not (I Jn. 16–17). Prayer on behalf of the sinner is sufficient to restore the latter, but not the former: *There is a sin that is mortal, I do not say you should pray about that.* The Matthean account of Jesus' teaching about fraternal correction also envisages a process of scrutiny by the Church in correcting wrongdoing (Mt. 18.15–20): if the wronged party cannot bring about reconciliation on his own, he is to take companions who will fulfil the Deuteronomic requirement for witnesses; if this fails, then the verdict of the whole Church prevails, with power to expel the contumacious party.

Moreover, the exercise of this power by an apostle is shown in Paul's treatment of a case of incest at Corinth. When he has condemned the man living with his mother-in-law as his wife, he tells the Corinthian Christians that they are to expel him, and to do so by declaring the spiritual penalty while gathered as the Church: *When you are assembled, and my spirit is present with the power of our Lord Jesus, you are to hand this man over to Satan for the destruction of the flesh, so that his spirit may be saved on the day of the Lord* (1 Cor. 5.4–5). Two principles therefore emerge: the gratuitous and complete forgiveness of sins which Baptism conveys to those who respond to the preaching of the gospel; and the authority of the Church to distinguish between types and cases of post-baptismal sin in judging whether individual sinners have forfeited their place in the assembly.

These two themes are brought together in the promise of Jesus to Peter and then to the other disciples in Matthew's gospel: *Truly I tell you, whatever you bind on earth will be bound in heaven, and whatever you loose on earth will be loosed in heaven* (Mt. 18.18). The forgiveness of sins which has been an integral characteristic of the preaching of Jesus and of his miracles of healing is to be perpetuated in the new economy of salvation of the Church: those who exercise his authority do so not simply as legislators or administrators, but as those who have his commission to relieve or maintain the consequences of human sinning. What is anticipated in the Matthean commission is made explicit in the Johannine account of the appearance of Christ to his disciples in the locked room on the evening of day of resurrection. There is a three-fold commission here: first, the disciples are instituted as the witnesses of the resurrection by the Lord's greeting of peace and the sight of his wounds; second, they are sent out on a mission which corresponds to the dynamic of the inner life of the Godhead, *As the Father has sent me, so I send you* (Jn. 20.21); third, they receive the Holy Spirit himself for the purpose of fulfilling this mission of reconciliation by the forgiveness of sins, *Receive the Holy Spirit. If you forgive the sins of any, they are forgiven them; if you retain the sins of any, they are retained* (Jn. 20.22). Because the forgiveness of sin is a divine power, the apostles need the infusion of the Holy Spirit in order to carry it out; because it is the Holy Spirit who acts in them to forgive sins, the effect of their binding and loosing is immediate and does not depend on any interval or intermediary to come into effect.

What is meant by the retention of sins? If sins are to be retained, then this cannot be a decision reached by chance or by prejudice or even by inspiration: the process has to be one of judging. And this act of judging is not simply one which on having weighed the circumstantial evidence of each case decides whether or not to remit the sin involved; it is an act which chooses between remission and binding, the imposition of a sanction which punishes the sin in a public way. So the forgiveness of sin is exercised by Christ in the Church in a way which is juridical, not because the freedom of forgiveness is to be confined to the human opinion of his ministers but because absolution has as its end not simply the personal spiritual healing and devotion of the penitent individual, but also the appropriate reconstitution of communion and order within the body of Christ, the re-enrolment of the sinner in the cultic community. For this to be effective, even the penitent Christian might be required to abstain from participation in the liturgy for a time, with or without other acts which demonstrate sorrow, so that the gravity of sin is marked and its forgiveness marked out as a conspicuous work of mercy and of grace: *Be merciful, just as your Father is merciful* (Lk. 6.36).

THE SACRAMENTAL CHARACTER OF RECONCILIATION

The Council of Trent called Penance a sacrament and defined it as instituted by the commission of Christ to the apostles in John 20, a power to be exercised by their successors and which is effective for the reconciliation of all sinners who have fallen after Baptism.[3] This was intended to contradict the teaching of Luther, who understood the power to forgive sin as a commission to preach, and so bring people to forgiveness through faith alone. But in what sense can repentance and forgiveness be made sacramental, when there appears to be no tangible sacramental sign attached to the power given? The scholastic analysis makes the act of absolution the form of the sacrament, and the penitent confession of mortal sin by the one seeking absolution its matter. The formula for absolution in the Latin Church is pronounced in the first person by the priest, which Thomas Aquinas explains as meaning not simply *I forgive you your sins in God's name*, but *I impart to you the sacrament of absolution*.[4]

122

This distinction is important: that God forgives the sin of those who are penitent if their circumstances make it impossible to receive sacramental absolution is certain, just as those who desire Baptism are considered to benefit from the grace which the sacrament gives even if they are deprived of its actual administration. However, just as the person baptised by desire must receive sacramental baptism if the opportunity arises before participating in the Eucharist, so those whose sin is forgiven by the act of true repentance which is called contrition still need reconciliation with the Church, in order to resume their role in the body of Christ conceived as a liturgical people. Where there is sin to be forgiven, the sacrament of absolution gives the sanctifying grace it signifies, because it is an effective sign, but the sign is not a material one like the water of Baptism but the act of reconciliation with the Church, which effects *ex opere operato* reconciliation with God.

In his treatment of sacramental penance, Leeming notes in particular how the administration of absolution in the patristic period was invariably expressed in terms of the relation of the penitent with the Church, and in particular the right either granted or denied to receive holy communion.[5] This is particularly apparent in Augustine, where reconciliation revivifies the sacramental graces given but left dormant through administration in schism, and achieves that peace of the Church which Christ himself attaches to the institution of the absolving ministry.[6] This ecclesial context rescues the ministry of absolution from what would otherwise be the caricature of an exponentially repeatable series of juridical interventions in the spiritual life of each individual penitent. The grace given in the sacrament forgives personal sin, but also repairs and re-establishes the integrity of the mystical body which is violated by that sin, so restoring the cultic holiness which the people of God enjoy by virtue of the perfect adorer who is their Head. Reconciliation with the Church is therefore not a simply human administrative process which is a necessary practical concomitant of divine forgiveness: it is the effective sign of reconciliation with God because *after absolution, the atonement made for sin avails not merely as an individual good act of the penitent, but also as united to the Church's power of atonement in union with Christ's.*[7]

SATISFACTION EXPRESSED AS CULT

This power of enhancement in communion with the Church is reflected in the treatment which Thomas Aquinas gives to the prayer which follows absolution in the traditional Latin rite: *Whatsoever good thou hast done, and every evil thou shalt have suffered, be unto thee for the remission of sins, and increase of grace and the reward of everlasting life.*[8] Although Thomas' account relies to some extent on the positivistic way in which he assumes the universal applicability of local liturgical practices, the insight which he articulates is already established in the controversies over penance that divided the African Church in the third century: that satisfaction for sin performed by the penitent has its value in and through its union with the Church's saving sacramental power. Thus the ecclesiastical penance which is generally conferred when absolution is given does not circum-scribe the capacity of the sinner to make amends, although it does express it in a formal sense. Rather, the entire life of the individual who is incorporated into Christ has the capacity to be united ecclesially in solidarity with the atoning work of the Cross, and complete *what is lacking in Christ's afflictions for the sake of his body, that is, the Church* (Col. 1.24). That this solidarity in reparation through sacramental re-enrolment in the liturgical people of God is a true act of cult was defended specifically by the Council of Trent: *If anyone says that the satisfactions by which penitents atone for their sins through Jesus Christ are not acts of worship of God, but are human traditions which obscure the teaching on grace, the true worship of God and the very benefit of the death of Christ: Let him be anathema.*[9]

124

The Tridentine treatment of satisfaction is emphatic that the works so performed have no efficacy apart from the incorporation of the individual performing them into the saving work of Christ: repentance which shows itself in reparative works has its value in restoring the destruction of human integrity and flourishing caused by sin, but its merit is simply that of Christ working in us, so that if we suffer with him, we will also be glorified with him (Rom. 8.17). This understanding of satisfaction when seen in an ecclesial and a christocentric context is a work of the virtue of religion: it remakes the Church which has been violated by sin, and so restores the cultic integrity which the designation of the people of God as priestly necessarily entails. But this remaking is entirely the consequence of the Pauline doctrine of incorporation into the fruits of the Passion: *I have been crucified with Christ; and it is no longer I who live but it is Christ who lives in me* (Gal. 2.19–20). The ceremony formerly known as the Absolution which took place at the end of the Requiem Mass in the historical Latin rite has now been suppressed, presumably because the title did not make clear that there is no juridical authority to absolve which the living possess that can be applied to the dead. However, by calling the rite an Absolution, the instinct of the older rite to express the Christian doctrine of satisfaction in terms of communion restated and restored is sound. The faithful departed who await the beatific vision are authentically incorporated into Christ even as they are prepared for heaven, and so the declaration of ecclesial solidarity made by the living Church with them through an absolution serves to revivify the satisfactory bond of communion.[10]

CHRISTIAN PENANCE AS FUNDAMENTALLY MEDICINAL, NOT JURIDICAL

How can this work of absolution, if it involves judging, not make of Christianity a religion of the law once again, in which the clergy administer a moral jurisprudence whose complexity and methods stand in stark contrast to the Christ who is *the end of the Law*? The Orthodox theologian Christos Yannaras writes critically of the Western tendency to codify canon law, which he considers is a baleful consequence of scholasticism in theological method and secularisation in seeking to imitate the legal codifications of post-revolutionary modern Europe. The canons of the Church which express the power of binding and loosing are not a statutory map of Christian living, nor a redefinition of Christian practice as unfree. He is emphatic that the fundamental characteristic of life in the Church is that of freedom: *when man is grafted into the Eucharistic mode of existence of the Church body, then no ready-made definition can correspond to the dynamism of the ways in which life is transfigured 'from glory to glory'. No casuistic subjection of man to objective provisions in laws or canons of life can exhaust the distinctiveness of the* name *given him by the Church within the communion and relation of love.*[11] However, the reality of the Church's life in communion has generated many canons and rules for conduct of her life, which deal with not only matters of administration and organisation, but also with the conditions by which the individual is judged as participating authentically in her life.

Yannaras grounds these canons in the fundamental category of martyrdom as exemplary and distinctive of the Church's life.[12] He notes that during the times of persecution before the peace of the Church all that was necessary to distinguish Christians from pagans by way of regulation were the four requirements of the apostolic council in Jerusalem (Acts 15.6–29). The constant possibility of martyrdom served as the supreme canon of the Church's life, marking the absolute distinction between life in Christ and life in the world. No further distinction was necessary, and all further canonical enactments have their force out of this fundamental norm of faithful witness even to death. This is because martyrdom is not simply a supreme act of heroism or self-denial, but rather the embodiment of the truth that transcending natural individuality through the love of Christ is the only way in which we can receive from him *the hypostasis of eternal life.*

The Church's canons are therefore at the service of self-transcendence, and have as their purpose *a witness to, and a possibility for, personal relationship with the whole body of the Church and the subjection of individuality to the common participation of all the faithful in oneness of the Church's life.*[13] Insofar as they achieve this, they serve the purpose of communion for which they exist; if they are not fundamentally orientated towards the supreme canon of martyrdom, and are in fact simply the expression of legislation in an ecclesiastical mode, *then their existence becomes a scandal in that it contradicts the gospel of salvation.*[14] The canons which express the Church's understanding of her power to bind and loose are thus fundamentally at the service of communion, because what they have as their end is to conform each Christian to the vocation of ecclesial martyrdom.

Yannaras considers the historical development of the canons in the period following the end of persecution and draws attention to the way in which the majority address issues of Church order rather than specific cases of individual behaviour. Even when the canon specifies removal from communion as a penalty for a particular action, as in the case of the marriage of monks and virgins considered by the Council of Chalcedon, the economy of freedom still gives to the bishop the right to exercise an appropriate clemency. In the East, it is in the aftermath of the Quinisext Council of 692 that canonical enactments dealing with individual conduct become numerous, just as in the West penitential codes with tariffs of penance began to emerge at the same time. Yannaras maintains that this does not mean the eclipse of martyrdom by codification: the canons preserve as their purpose what the council calls *the cure of souls and the healing of passions,* and thus have a primary orientation towards healing and restoration within the Body of Christ.[15] This process is fundamentally ascetic: in order to disengage the Christian from perceiving the purpose of living in purely natural terms, the Church needs to propose objective standards and aids to self-knowledge which demonstrate *the existential failure and condemnation represented by the autonomy of ... individuality.*[16] To this self-knowledge is added in the imposition of particular penances what Yannaras calls *a measure of the Church's ascetic consciousness:*[17] submission to the canons as a recognition of our distance from the authentic life of the Church is in itself an act of participation in the Church's delineation of spiritual failure, and the principal step towards a restoration of communion and life.

Yannaras therefore sees the existence of canonical penance as medicinal and ascetic, not juridical and meritorious. He welcomes the obsolete character of many of the canons and the lack of system which the Eastern collections exhibit precisely because this illustrates their nature as occasional, the precipitation of the Church's sacramental and penitential life in a particular time and place.[18] However, his ecclesiology does not allow the Church any hypostatic reality other than the Eucharistic assembly, despite whatever legal or administrative arrangements might accidentally appear to govern her social role, and as such the *locus* of the communion which the Eucharistic community realises must be not a juridical 'person' but the fatherhood of the bishop. This entrustment of the principle of communion to the oversight of an individual does not appeal to the modern mentality which conceives of freedom as personal autonomy and prefers the intervention of laws to the supervision of a person. But despite the sins of bishops which Yannaras does not hesitate to call the *ultimate hazard* of the Church,[19] the personal mode of salvation to which the Church gives her witness cannot be expressed by an ecclesiology that substitutes laws, codes, charters and covenants for the authentic *personal adventure of freedom and repentance.*[20] Yannaras is obviously unsympathetic to the scholastic understanding of satisfaction and merit, but in his account of the purpose of the Church's canons he is not distant from the fundamental principle of absolution and penance as the reviviscence of ecclesial life through the solidarity of restored communion which characterises the reformed Western doctrine defined at Trent.

Yannaras' insistence on the person of the bishop rather than the inanimate body of canon law as the principle of ecclesial communion emphasises the Orthodox ideal of a spiritual economy which resorts to canons on an occasional basis to delineate the boundaries of communion, but places the principal emphasis on the sympathetic spiritual fatherhood whose archetype is the bishop but which exists in parallel to the hierarchy through the tradition of ascetic eldership characteristic of the Eastern Churches. This elision of corrective discipline, pastoral care and spiritual oversight develops simultaneously in the West, as public penance gives way to private confession. However, there is a fundamental theological turn in the Western tradition which transforms the character as well as the practice of penance and with it the role of the priests who exercise the ministry of forgiveness. The canonical system of penance as it existed from the patristic period applied sanctions to acts: the virgin who marries, the priest who is drunk, the adulterous husband each incur a penalty when the sin is proved and the community headed by the bishop adjudicates the penance. The archetypal guide to the cure of souls in the West, Gregory the Great's *Regula Pastoralis*, largely consists of a list of different sinners whose admonition is the pastor's primary duty.

THE ECLIPSE OF THE PUBLIC CHARACTER OF RECONCILIATION IN THE WEST

The development of ethical thought in the West, in particular by Abelard in the eleventh century, introduced the principle of motive and consent, with momentous consequences.

Theologians, and so the confessors who looked to them for instruction, now added to the customary gradations of acts to which penalties were attached considerations of intention and circumstance. This inevitably made the administration of sacramental penance both more forensic and more intimate: when use of the sacrament was made compulsory on an annual basis in 1215,[21] the need of the clergy to acquire this new competence was supplied by the emergence of manuals which in conception and method persisted until the mid-twentieth century.

Two consequences followed from this: first, the practice of the devout to confess frequently and without any consciousness of mortal sin, the sacramental validity of which remained contentious until modern times; and second, the use of the sacrament to inculcate spiritual progress in the life of prayer by skilled confessors. The exclusion of a rigorist Augustinianism from the administration of penance with the condemnation of Jansenism, and the emergence of a 'golden mean' out of the thickets of casuistical moral theology based on the working practice of the Italian John Wesley, S. Alphonsus de Liguori, meant that the delay in granting absolution until amendment of life was secure and penance done which was once prevalent disappeared almost entirely. In the Latin Church penance largely resolved itself into the invariable granting of absolution after each confession, with only a residual formal penance being given on each occasion, the focus of strictly penitential interest having shifted to the acquisition of indulgences.

THE PRACTICE OF PENANCE IN ANGLICANISM

This pattern (without the interest in indulgences) was the one inherited by the leaders of the Oxford Movement when they sought to restore the practice of sacramental confession as integral to the life of the English Church, and they looked to contemporary continental practice as a guide. They inherited

in *The Book of Common Prayer* aspirations which by the second
quarter of the nineteenth century were largely defunct and
ripe for renewal. The Prayer Book mentions public penance in
the preface of the Commination service, in which it commends
the godly discipline, that at the beginning of Lent, such persons as stood
convicted of sin were put to open penance, and punished in this world,
that their souls might be saved in the day of the Lord. In place of
this defunct discipline, the restoration of which *is much to be*
wished, the ritual cursing of sinners is proposed. However, an
extensive and controversial system of moral oversight using
Churchwardens to present offenders and Church courts to
enforce discipline existed with some vigour and used excom-
munication as its principal means of enforcing reform, a
penalty which largely lost its sanction when the principal civil
disabilities attendant on it were abolished in 1813. The Canons
of 1604 which establish and regulate this procedure make an
exception however for those cases in which the minister of the
parish discovers such offences because of a confession made to
him of *secret and hidden sins, for the unburdening of . . . conscience and*
to receive spiritual consolation and ease of mind.[22] These crimes and
offences are to remain secret. The Prayer Book mentions two
occasions on which such a confession might be made: first, in
the second Exhortation in the Communion Office, those of
unquiet conscience are encouraged to open their grief, and
so receive *the benefit of absolution, together with ghostly counsel and*
advice; and second, in the office for *The Visitation of the Sick*, the
Minister is to move the sick person to make a confession, and
absolve him or her using the typical first-person Latin-rite
formula.

It is apparent that although the principal controversial
Anglican divines were insistent that compulsory confession
was neither scriptural nor necessary, the classic doctrine of
absolution as efficacious by its own power and not simply
as a prayer or declaration was preserved. John Cosin writes
typically in controversy: *The truth is, that in the Priest's absolution*

there is the true power and virtue of forgiveness, which will most certainly take effect, Nisi ponitur obex, *as in Baptism.*[23] Habitual (if very occasional) resort to auricular confession and absolution remained the practice of some Anglicans long enough for its memory to be significant in the opening controversies of the Oxford Movement.[24] Absolution as part of the parish priest's responsibilities to the dying was evidently sufficiently well established in popular expectation to merit its mention in *Tom Jones*, when the apparent death-bed conversion of Squire Western to rationalistic deism so infuriates Dr Thwackum; the difficulty of imagining a similar scene in either Jane Austen or Dickens perhaps indicates a meaningful shift of pastoral practice among Anglican Christians.

The Tractarian revival of private confession and absolution was therefore able to draw on a secure body of authorised post-Reformation provision in the Anglican formularies to justify itself, but not much actual pastoral practice. The inclusion of texts for general confession and absolution using declaratory formulae to communicate the forgiveness of sins in the various public offices of the Prayer Book added a further complexity to the enunciation of a consistent doctrine of absolution in the Church of England. The revival of the practice of sacramental confession and the employment of contemporary Roman Catholic manuals by clergy anxious to exercise this ministry provoked the inevitable outrage of Protestants and ineffective efforts at suppression, regulation and censure.[25]

The discipline established itself among the Tractarians and their followers much as Dr Pusey himself taught and used it: for the forgiveness of sins, devout use of the general confessions provided by the Prayer Book in public worship sufficed, but the authentic administration of a sacramental absolution required the contents of an auricular confession as its matter. It is a remarkable testimony to the spiritual vitality of the Oxford Movement that the practice of private confession on an habitual basis established itself so widely in the Church of England, even though the official organs of teaching throughout the period insisted on its entirely voluntary character, and denied that the clergy had any right to insist on it, question a penitent generally about sins committed, or act in any way which appeared to constrain the freedom of the one confessing to open his grief as he or she saw fit.

The consequence of this for Anglican pastoral practice had been odd. Because of the discontinuity between the post-Reformation insular tradition, such as it was, and the revival of private confession and absolution encouraged by the Oxford Movement, the technique of confession for both priest and penitent was drawn largely and perhaps unwittingly from the pastoral practice of nineteenth century Roman Catholicism, but without admitting the principle of the necessity of sacramental absolution for the forgiveness of grave sin on which it is based. The benefit of this for souls seeking to deepen their spiritual life has been very great, particularly as the relatively small proportion of Anglican communicants who made use of the sacrament enabled those who heard confessions to take great pains in encouraging and advising their penitents. But the so-called confession of devotion, in which the individual uses the sacrament to confess venial sins and seek spiritual advice, is for lay Christians at least the product of Counter-Reformation piety, and has suffered as much in Anglicanism as in Roman Catholicism from the collapse of these devotional habits in the aftermath of the Second Vatican Council. The ecclesial dimension of confession and absolution, by which the sinner is reincorporated into the liturgical assembly as the efficacious sign of forgiveness after repentance ironically disappeared from England with the eclipse of public penance just before the advent of the Oxford Movement, and no system of internal discipline reflecting the denominational character and membership of the Church of England in modern society has taken its place.

THE UNIQUE SACRAMENTAL CHARACTER
OF THE VIRTUE OF PENITENCE

The nature of penitence in the Christian life is distinctive
because it is a virtue given a sacramental character. This
dual identity arises because in the sacrament of absolution the
outward sign is not a material thing but a human act, the act
of renouncing sin and receiving ecclesial pardon, and as such
can be virtuous. But the character of penitence as a virtue is
complex: it relates most particularly to justice, because it has
as its object human acts and the commutation of punishment
due for acts committed by a free choice to make amends. But
as Thomas Aquinas points out, *inasmuch as there is a justice of man
towards God, it must have a share in matter pertaining to the theological
virtues, the object of which is God.*[26] Penitence therefore includes
faith in the Passion of Christ as the source of forgiveness, hope
in the pardon which God grants through it, and the hatred of
sin which derives from Christian charity. In its relation to the
cardinal virtues, it is directed by prudence, and as a portion
of commutative justice giving each his due it inspires the
Christian to be temperate in the use of pleasure and coura-
geous in the endurance of hardship. It is not the same as the
emotion of shame, because to be ashamed is a reaction to an
evil act as present, not a resolution of the will to address the
evil act as past and in need of amendment. Aquinas gives as the
definition of the virtue of penitence *a supernatural habit infused
by God whereby man readily inclines both to sorrow for sins committed
inasmuch as they offend God and to a firm purpose of amendment.*[27]

The foundation therefore of the raising of penitence to be
sacramental is the virtuous act of will which arises from the
demand of justice, but which embraces the entire economy
of the Christian moral life infused in Baptism insofar as it
relates to what is required for the forgiveness of sin by God.
This virtue manifests itself in acts which express its character:
hatred of sin; sorrow for having offended God; the desire to

destroy the presence of sin in us; the desire to make amends to God for having sinned; and the intention to live free from sin in the future. Because it is a virtue which is common to all those redeemed from sin, it is not extinguished by the vision of God in heaven, but remains as a joyful thanksgiving for satisfaction made and justice fulfilled.

The preaching of the gospel presents the virtue of repentance as the essential prerequisite for the forgiveness of sins: *repent therefore, and turn to God so that your sins may be wiped out* (Acts 3.19). This repentance does not consist only in ceasing from sin and resolving to lead a new life; sorrow for past sin remains, and serves to strengthen the spirit of penitence against relapse, as S. Gregory the Great writes, *to do penance is to weep for our evil deeds, and weeping not to perpetrate them again.*[28] The distinctive character of Christian penitence as a virtue is its assumption into the cultic structure of the moral life of the baptised by the institution of sacramental absolution: the ministerial priesthood exercises in the name of Christ reconciliation, in order that the cultic integrity of the people of God as holy and intended for beatitude might be restored.

SACRAMENTAL RECONCILIATION RESTORES THE CHRISTIAN TO LITURGICAL CULT

The sacramental structure of penance has as its efficacious signification the act of repentance made by the penitent in making confession of sin and the act of the priest in administering the act of absolution; this signification makes sacramental the repentance which the sinner expresses as a consequence of the operation of the virtue of penitence, and effects the forgiveness of sin, which is the reality signified by the outward action taken as a whole. For this forgiveness to take effect, the sinner must be contrite: that is, must have sorrow and hatred for sin committed, a firm resolve not to sin again, and an intention to make satisfaction for past sins.

135

Because this sacramental absolution has as its outward sign the reconciliation of the individual sinner to the Church after Baptism, the confession of sin needs to relate to the individual instances by which the baptismal integration of the individual into the Church is harmed, and cannot simply be generic: this requirement is not simply a devotional technique to stimulate sorrow, or a commodification of sin which obscures the depravity of our fallen nature; it is an acknowledgement of the failure of communion which sin causes, both in our communion with Christ who is head of the Church and our communion with its members as delegated to cult.

MINISTERIAL PRIESTHOOD AS EVANGELICAL IN RESTORING THE PENITENT CHRISTIAN

It is the minister of the Church who needs both order and juris-diction to absolve authentically, who effects this reconciliation in the name of the whole body, and in doing so causes the sin confessed to be forgiven as the outward sign of penance takes place. This possession of jurisdiction in the technical sense is not a juridical requirement imposed on the free offer of forgiveness to its detriment. It is the recognition that to reconcile with the Church the minister needs to speak and act authentically in her name, and that ordination without a cure of souls is not enough to constitute this authenticity. However, the possession of priestly ordination and the requisite authority to absolve do not exhaust the evangelical qualities which the confessor needs to possess. The priest needs right judgement, prudence and knowledge to fulfil the role of teaching, warning and encour-agement to conversion which the reconciliation of penitents demands. This demonstrates the personal character of the bond of communion which Christos Yannaras emphasises as the authentic Christian counterpart to secular juridical structures.[29]

It is through the submission of one's own judgement to that of another who stands as the reconciling representative of the Eucharistic community that the penitent is freed from the solipsistic autonomy of sin and re-incorporated into a communion which gives life through deification. This deification can only take place when the Christian has the courage to embrace eternal life, and the act of absolution restores in the Christian the baptismal image of Christ and so the resolution to lay down life in order that it might be saved. Because this is a personal re-enrolment in the liturgy of deification, it cannot but take place in a personal encounter, in which the priest acts as the judge who is also physician and counsellor, according to the integrity of the person of the glorified Christ whose priestly ministry is thus exercised.

THE RESTORATION OF COMMUNION
COMMON TO THE PRACTICE OF PENANCE

The practice of penance and the administration of absolution in the Christian Church have varied as much as the circumstances of Christians have changed: the public penance of the early Church, in which the bishop declares the canonical verdict of the Eucharistic community over which he presides on the acts of her members, appears to inhabit a different moral world from the intense, devotional ethos of Tractarian confessional practice. To these changes in human sensibility are added the intense theological controversies which have surrounded the exercise of this ministry: the rigorism of those who excluded penance for mortal sins; the Reformation repudiation of penance and satisfaction as works inimical to justification by faith alone; the Jansenist exaggeration of authentic contrition into a state virtually unachievable by the ordinary Christian; the collapse of the confession of devotion in the wake of the crisis of conventional piety following the Second Vatican Council.

However, the sacramental character of absolution as a rite which places the forgiveness of sin in an ecclesial context remains fundamental in defining the Christian character as both free from the law and delegated to cultic holiness. Because absolution is sacramental and not legal, it is able to forgive post-baptismal sin, while identifying that its fundamental malice lies not in the violation of a code of precepts but in the extinction of authentic communion. The principle of meritorious satisfaction to be made for past sin is an enhancement of this sense of communion, because it elevates the goodness of virtuous living into the context of reparative ecclesial life, while at the same time ascribing the worth of such living only to the infused moral headship of Christ.

The commission of Christ to the apostles to forgive sin given after the resurrection is a commission accompanied by the gift of the Holy Spirit, and the absolving sign of reconciliation with the Church only has the power and virtue of forgiving sins because it is the work of the Spirit within the soul of the Christian. But the concomitant presence of the Spirit as the one whose seven-fold gifts illuminate and complete the virtuous crown of Christian moral living means that the gift of absolution, because personal, is accompanied by the compassionate sympathy of the pastor for the penitent, the quality of spiritual eldership. Christian priesthood is not fulfilled in ritual observance, because its character is determined by that of Christ himself, *who knows our weaknesses*. But the ritual character of absolution as an act of the Church performed by one ordained to effect communion by the celebration of the Eucharist places the mystery of the forgiveness of sins within the cultic life of the people of God, and so within the religious moral orientation which anticipates deification and beatitude. Through the virtue of penitence the Christian is enabled to turn from sin and make amends for it through sorrow and reparation; when this penitence is given a sacramental character through the act of absolution, it becomes a repentance which receives through restored communion a moral and sacral solidarity with the life of the whole Church, and so lives infused with all the merits of the one who is her Head.

Notes for Chapter 6

1 Fielding, Henry, *Tom Jones*, p 214.
2 *ST, Suppl* q 38 a 5.
3 Council of Trent, Session 14, Canons 1, 3 concerning the most holy sacrament of penance in Tanner & Alberigo, *Decrees*, vol 2 p 711–12.
4 *ST*, III q 84 a 3.
5 Leeming, Bernard, *Sacramental Theology*, p 361–3.
6 Leeming, *Sacramental Theology*, p 362.
7 Leeming, *Sacramental Theology*, p 264.
8 Aquinas, Thomas, *Questiones de quodlibet*, 3 q 13 a 28.
9 Council of Trent, Session 14, canon 14 concerning the most holy sacrament of penance in Tanner & Alberigo, *Decrees*, vol 2 p 713.
10 The collect of the rite states: *Absolve, O Lord, we beseech thee, the soul of thy servant from every bond of sin: that in the glory of the resurrection he with thy saints and elect, may rise to a new and better life.*
11 Yannaras, Christos, *The Freedom of Morality*, p 173.
12 Yannaras, *The Freedom of Morality*, p 177–8.
13 Yannaras, *The Freedom of Morality*, p 178.
14 Yannaras, *The Freedom of Morality*, p 178.
15 Yannaras, *The Freedom of Morality*, p 180.
16 Yannaras, *The Freedom of Morality*, p 181.
17 Yannaras, *The Freedom of Morality*, p 181.
18 Yannaras, *The Freedom of Morality*, p 184.
19 Yannaras, *The Freedom of Morality*, p 192–3.
20 Yannaras, *The Freedom of Morality*, p 193.
21 Lateran Council IV, Constitution 21 *Omnis utriusque sexus* in Tanner & Alberigo, *Decrees*, vol 1 p 245.
22 *Constitutions and Canons Ecclesiastical 1604*, Canon 113.
23 Cosin, John, given in More, Paul & Cross, F Leslie, *Anglicanism*, p 515.
24 See Nockles, Peter, *The Oxford Movement in Context*, pp 248–56.

25 Most notably the controversy over the manual *The Priest in Absolution* published privately for the use of members of the Society of the Holy Cross in 1866.

26 *ST*, III q 85 a 5.

27 *ST*, III q 85 a 2.

28 Gregory the Great, *Gospel Homily*, 34.

29 Yannaras, *The Freedom of Morality*, pp 189–92.

Conclusion

How might Christian faith and practice be invigorated if its character as a religion were to be seen unambiguously as virtuous and its ethical imperative as encapsulated in a cultic setting? Hooker's enthusiasm for the moral rectitude of religion in the right ordering of the Church's place in the Christian commonwealth emphasises the importance of a tangible landscape of consecration and devotion, which is physical, even topographical, and temporal. Attentiveness to this patrimony, and energy expended for its renovation and where necessary restoration, is a characteristic mark of the self-renewing Catholic vitality which makes Anglicans such mercurial ecumenical partners for the other reformed traditions of these islands, and which insistently draws them to their own hermeneutic of continuity with the pre-reformation inheritance of the *Ecclesia Anglicana*. However, there is a loss of nerve in contemporary English Anglicanism which perceives all too well that the practice of the Christian faith has not been re-vitalised or even sustained by forty years of drastic liturgical revision, and that those parish churches which seem to be most flourishing are those which often have least interest in preserving anything but the most tangential purchase on the shape and content of traditional Anglican piety.

EXTERNAL CULT AS A PREREQUISITE
FOR CHRISTIAN MISSION

This loss of nerve has been canonised by the extraordinary status now given to any manifestation of Christian practice within the institutional ambit of the Church of England which can successfully brand itself as a 'Fresh Expression': rites and texts, the consecrated character of the parish church and the exclusive cure which attaches to it, all appear dispensable, if by abandoning them a chimerical aspiration to increase numbers of participants in certain sorts of communal faith activity might be secured. It seems irrelevant that in pursuit of this aim the vitality of the vast bulk of the institution which remains outside this zareba of enthusiasts has the practices which sustain it deconstructed as allegedly termi- nally ineffectual for the purposes of contemporary mission. The Church of England has never been a *Volkskirche* in the sense that the Scandinavian Lutheran Churches once were, precisely because in its insistence on the virtuous character of religious practice conceived as reverent external cult it failed to convince a substantial minority of English people that it was sufficiently reformed, and was content that this be so rather than sacrifice this fundamental grounding of its identity.

A renewed sense of religion as a virtue which orientates Christians towards beatitude, rather than as the depot of redundant formalism, is an absolutely necessary prerequisite for Catholic reviviscence, in which the local epicentres of pastoral care have at their heart a consecrated house, in which the transcendent moral vocation of those incorporated into Christ is realised in the *pietas* of authentic cult. It is also a necessary antidote to the all too persistent peremptory reduc- tionism which remains endemic in the liturgical practice of Western Catholicism, by which the subordination of religion to justice makes of worship simply the discharge of a debt required by the law of what is owed to God himself.

THE SACRAMENTAL CHARACTER
OF AUTHENTIC CULT

This re-pristinating work of religion as virtue draws its vitality from the sacramental economy, in which Christ, whose incarnation is the fundamental mystery, perpetuates his presence through signs which are both exemplary and effective. The intelligibility of the sacramental order to which Augustine draws attention grounds each sacramental sign in this fundamental mystery, and through them endows the well-disposed Christian with the supernatural vitality of the resurrection, in which Christ's various perfections each have a saving *impetus* of grace. This role is a medicinal one: the lost image of God is restored in fallen humanity and so the redeemed Christian is incorporated into the liturgical structure of salvation history, in which perfect worship is now offered to the Father. This perfect worship is the work of his Son, as priest and victim, and is pre-eminently carried out in the consecration of the Eucharistic sacrifice, which re-capitulates the offering of Calvary and in so doing sacramentally embeds the temporal act of propitiation in the concomitant presence of the glorified Christ. The Christian religion possesses at the heart of its sacramental economy a sacrifice which elevates the ritual act of commemoration in the Lord's Supper to that of a universal suffrage, in which the living and the departed, the present and the absent, are united in the impetrative immolation of the Cross. Given this premise, the Church is only intelligible in her mission if the sacramental principle informs her entire life, and if the Eucharistic oblation which is its summit sanctifies the people of God by the centrality and dignity of its offering.

This cannot be realised if the value of sacramental participation is reduced to a moral and pedagogical one, and if the work of offering is understood as the visible community realising by its work a mysterious benefit, rather than the community itself becoming truly liturgical by its enrolment in the high priestly work of Christ. Here the Thomist physicalist explanation of sacramental efficacy has practical consequences of the highest importance. Ethical sacramentalism contributes to secularisation by mortgaging the liturgical environment to the presumed ethos of the gathered community, from which usually follows a debilitating constriction of cultic resource. Confidence in the instrumental effectiveness of the sacramental dispensation, provided it avoids converting this tangibility into a commodified fulfilment of obligation, gives to the liturgical formation of the people of God not an opportunity for facile activity but a much more profound initiation into the fundamental mystery of the Gospel, in which Christ conforms them to his own character as perfect adorer. The emphasis placed on active participation by the people in liturgical rites which has played so significant a part in the revision of the Roman rite since the Second Vatican Council cannot simply be accepted without question as meaning that the pedagogic and psychological affectivity of the gathered congregation must always and in every case be given a privileged position in determining how sacramental worship is to be ordered. Active participation is the work of Christ who enrols the Christian, and is thus liturgically delegated to cult; it is not the work of Christians who evoke Christ by their own empathetic activity.

SACRAMENTAL CHARACTER AND LITURGICAL HEADSHIP

This enrolment for cult is the way in which the ethical life becomes conformed to adoration, and the Christian people become designated as an authentic priesthood. The reception of this character of priesthood by the baptised is explained by Thomas Aquinas exclusively in terms of the expectation of glory and the carrying on of the worship of God: the ethical traction of beatitude configures the Christian to the sacramental sacrifice of the new covenant. However, the fact of incorporation into this priesthood does not give to the baptised Christian the ministerial character of a priest. This ministerial character derives from the call of Christ to be conformed to his priesthood in the sacramental order, which is a commission in particular to consecrate the Eucharistic sacrifice and forgive sins by means of reconciliation with the Church. These acts undertaken specifically in his name and as a consequence of his explicit institution are confined in their exercise to the episcopate and to the presbyterate: the former as succeeding to the apostolic exercise of headship in the liturgical assembly, the latter as their delegates. This headship is not simply administrative or pastoral, although it encompasses both roles: it is liturgical, in the sense that the celebration of the sacramental sacrifice enrols each Christian according to charism and order. Indeed, there is a particularly close relationship between the exercise of Eucharistic presidency and the reconciliation of the penitent: the one who oversees the sacramental realisation of the people of God as designated for glory in the Eucharist is the one who restores the sinner with medicinal compassion. This ministerial priesthood is definitive because it depends wholly on the action of Christ, who as perfect adorer (not perfect penitent) offers the only acceptable worship, and who in his person delineates authentic ministry on behalf of his body just as on the Cross he delineates authentic sacrifice.

The emphasis on the doctrine of character as it relates to ordination, which in both Tridentine and Anglican polemic secured at the Reformation the necessary theological rigour to preserve the conventional shape of the three-fold ministry, is now jeopardised by the incipient collapse of the devotional and social superstructure which supported the clergy as a professional caste. The eclipse of this model, and the reticence of many of the ordained to distinguish their ministry from that of the active and educated laity on whom they now often largely depend in carrying out their pastoral office should

145

not be allowed to obscure the fundamental importance of the *signaculum* of ordination. It is a manifestation of Christ himself as priest and minister, the indelibility of which is a consecration to the service of the people of God whose covenantal priesthood is conceived as a sacramental economy of grace and communion.

LITURGICAL REFORM AND BEATITUDE

Attention to inculcating religion as the informing virtue of cult requires attention to rite, which manifests the mystery of Christ as the foundation of the sacramental order. Contemporary liturgical practice has been afflicted by a variety of unsatisfactory theological influences which have made necessary and overdue reforms anaemic and disappointing when applied pastorally. In particular this arises from an ethical interpretation of sacramental efficacy which wrongly identifies the congregation as the subject of liturgical work; a persistent and costive legalism which reduces religious rite to the performance of a quantifiable duty; a Kantian suspicion of the aesthetic, which has eclipsed the Augustinian appreciation of beauty as properly transcendent; an exclusion of anagogical reference which neglects the concomitant presence of Christ as glorified in the sacramental sacrifice. These theological assumptions are not the inevitable inspiration of rites which have been reformed to accommodate and encourage the active participation of the laity, whose renewed visibility in the celebration of the liturgy is essentially a fruit of the renewal of moral theology, a renewal moreover which took place in resolutely unreformed liturgical atmosphere of baroque Italy.

It is evident that the contemporary trend in liturgical reform in the Latin Church is towards the preservation of the essential participatory characteristics of the rites reformed after the Second Vatican Council, but re-sacralised through the parallel use of the older liturgical books, and by emphasising continuities of vesture, language, music and architecture with the historic Roman rite. The key reform is the return to Eastward-facing celebration of the Eucharist, which would restore the appropriate sacred space proper to the eschatological hope proclaimed in the sacramental act. The Anglican experience is important here, firstly in the restoration of altars themselves, and then in the adoption of Eastward-facing celebration under the influence of successive Catholic revivals. Without this, the great majority of church buildings built before the recent reform will continue to project a depressing visual discontinuity in their sanctuaries, the very place where the tradition recognises in the altar the primary Christological image of the entire liturgy. Nor should any explanation of the meaning of the Eucharistic sacrifice as determined by the signs which effect it exclude ritual practice which anticipates the beatific vision. Christ's oblation is made under the sign of a ritual meal, but his necessary and concomitant presence is not exhausted in its meaning by this signification, and it remains a sound and authentic liturgical instinct to express this in a sacral anticipation of the worship of the Apocalypse. Iconoclasm not only compromises the substantive reality of the incarnation by its refusal of the sacred in art: it is a denial of the anagogical principle, an exclusion of beatitude from the temporal liturgy and so the possibility of an authentic cultic formation for the vision of God. Religious rite must not collude with iconoclasm by extinguishing the notion of consecration from time, place, object and gesture: the offering of sacrifice has its own approved practice, and if this is recognised in the aspirations of natural religion, how much more so where *faith, the outward sense befriending, makes the inward vision clear.*[1]

RECONCILIATION AS AUTHENTICALLY CULTIC

The sacramental forgiveness of sins which is reconciliation with the Church through the absolving ministry of its priests

is a rite which finds itself to a large degree in contemporary
crisis: habits of devotion which sustained frequent confession
during the early part of the Liturgical Movement among Latin
Christians have now dissipated, partly because of dissent over
particular moral norms, and partly because the characteristic
piety of the nineteenth century Catholic revival is superseded.
This eclipse of the confession of devotion has had important
consequences for Anglicanism, where the penitential superstructure the Tractarians erected on the somewhat exiguous
foundation of The Book of Common Prayer has suffered the
same fate as the continental sources from which they drew.
This does not detract from the importance which Anglicans
continue to attach to the general confessions followed by
a ministerial absolution which so characterise their rites.
However, given that compulsory annual confession was only
firmly established in the West in 1215, and has never been
required consistently among the Orthodox Churches, the
value and efficacy of sacramental penance cannot depend on
the particular way in which it has taken juridical form since
then.

The classic Western formulation of what happens in sacramental penance absolutely secures the rite in the medicinal
work of restoring communion: the absolution itself makes the
requisite outward sign reconciliation of the penitent with the
Church and re-enrolment in the liturgical community; the
satisfaction which the penitent offers in response to this is not
the commutation of a debt but an act of cult, in which a reparative work signifies the act of Christ within and for the sinner.
The Latin ecclesiastical vocabulary of merit, satisfaction
and indulgences is unfortunate here in trying to convey the
solidarity in communion which sacramental absolution and
its concomitant assumption of reparation into cult achieves:
if it can be detached from its Chaucerian overtones, the
word 'pardon' expresses much better what is meant and
done. Because the sacramental economy is instituted to be

medicinal, sacramental absolution has a bias for pardon, and here the insight of Yannaras that the discipline of the Church consists fundamentally in the canon of martyrdom and the oversight of the chief liturgist as the ascetic conscience of the Eucharistic community is a necessary corrective to the urge to codify penance. The virtue of penitence which Christ raises to a sacramental dignity in the rite of absolution cannot be quantified in terms of what the sinner owes, which is why the act of satisfaction which the sinner makes to acknowledge responsibility for spiritual failure is so aptly elevated by the sacrament from an unpayable debt to an act of religion in Christ. This fundamental freedom of Christian morality binds the exercise of the priest's ministry in overseeing reconciliation to clemency, so that in the act of forgiveness the community of faith might be restored with acts that glorify God.

RELIGION AND THE RECOVERY OF PRIESTHOOD

The understanding of Christianity as a religion for which this book has argued, in which the Christian receives a vocation to holiness which is infused and sustained by sacramental worship, and in which the ministerial priesthood continues through sacramental sacrifice and sacramental forgiveness the work of Jesus Christ as perfect adorer, proposes an ecclesiology which is fundamentally cultic and anagogical. These are not themes which sit easily with much contemporary Christian self-understanding, where activism, didacticism and a lack of what the scholastics called purgatorial fortitude in thinking about the last things are all too evident in what informs liturgical and pastoral preferences for many clergy. Happy puritans are not people of cult. This intense ethicism ironically misses the fundamental role of religion as the virtue which orientates the moral life towards the promise of glory, and substitutes for this authentic liturgical enrolment the moral *impetus* which the community itself aspires to generate. It is not surprising that in these settings sacramental practice is eclipsed and the character of ministerial priesthood either denied or ignored. But this represents a profound secularisation, a violent expulsion from the temporal environment in which human beings practise their faith of its final end, and the character of that final end as a communion of saints. Christian cult serves as a preservative of the eschatological vocation of the Church, in which sacred buildings, rites and habits virtuously map out on the landscape of the earthly city the incursion of beatitude.

On the feast of Pentecost the apostles receive the gift of the Holy Spirit with the visible sign of tongues as of fire, and their preaching restores the communion lost to the human race in the confusion of Babel. In the Western Church the vestments worn to celebrate this feast are red, with an obvious symbolism; for the Byzantine Slavs, however, the colour is green. The descent of the Spirit on the Church is always the well-spring of her fecundity, the renewal of all that is fruitful and the inspiration of all that is of Christ. Renewal in the Church is fidelity to the work of the Spirit, not confidence in our own capacity to achieve it. It is the Holy Spirit whom Christ breathes onto the apostles when he appoints them to be the merciful ministers of reconciliation; it is the gift of the Spirit which Timothy is urged to fan into a flame when he is ordained by the laying on of hands for the oversight of the people of God; it is the Holy Spirit whose invocation consecrates the sacramental sacrifice according to the rite of the oriental liturgies, and so makes tangible the communion which the apostle calls His own. Christian priesthood is the ministry which serves the people of God from the wellsprings of grace appointed by Christ and made abundantly fruitful by the abiding presence of the Spirit, the spring-time of the Church. In the vision of Ezekiel it is the renewed Temple which waters the land and makes it fruitful and consecrated: the cult which nourishes with life; the adoration which does not fail; the cleansing river which saves.

Note for Conclusion

1 S. Thomas Aquinas, from the hymn *Pange Lingua, gloriosi*, in the Office of Corpus Christi, translated by Edward Caswall.

Bibliography

Biblical references are given from *The Holy Bible, New Revised Standard Version, Anglicized edition* (Oxford 1995).

Aquinas, Thomas, *Expositio in evangelium Ioannis* (two volumes, Turin, 1953)

Aquinas, Thomas, from the hymn *Pange Lingua, gloriosi*, in the office of Corpus Christi, translated by Edward Caswall.

Aquinas, Thomas, *Questiones de Quodlibet* (Turin, 1949)

Aquinas, Thomas, *Questiones disputate de veritate*, translated by Mulligan, Robert as *Truth* (three volumes, Indianapolis, 1954, 1994)

Aquinas, Thomas, *Summa Theologica*, translated by the Fathers of the English Dominican Province (five volumes, New York, 1948, 1981)

Augustine, *Answer to Faustus, a Manichaean*, translated by Teske, Ronald and edited by Ramsey, Boniface (New York, 2007)

Augustine, *City of God*, translated by Bettenson, Henry (London, 1984)

Augustine, *Contra Epistulam Parmeniani*, edited by J-P Migne, *Patrologia Latina* 43, 33–108

Augustine, *De Baptismo*, Library of Nicene and Post-Nicene Fathers, first series, volume four (Edinburgh, 1887)

Augustine, *Enchiridion*, edited by Scheel, Otto (Tübingen, 1937)

Augustine, *Select Letters*, Library of Nicene and Post-Nicene Fathers, first series, volume one (Edinburgh, 1886)

Barker, Margaret, *Temple Theology: An Introduction* (London, 2004)

Barker, Margaret, *The Hidden Tradition of the Kingdom of God* (London, 2007)

Berger, David, *Thomas Aquinas and the Liturgy* (Naples, Florida, 2004)

Bérulle, Pierre de, *Opuscules de Piété* (Grenoble, 1997)

The Book of Common Prayer (Oxford, Cambridge, 1662)

Butler, Christopher, *The Theology of Vatican II* (revised edition, London, 1981)

Cajetan, Thomas, The commentary of Thomas de Vio, Cardinal Cajetan is printed in the Leonine edition of the *Summa Theologiae* (Rome, 1888–1906)

Casel, Odo, *The Mystery of Christian Worship, and other writings* (London, 1962)

Catechism of the Catholic Church (London, 1994)

Chrysostom, John, *Homilies on the Epistle to the Ephesians*, Library of Nicene and Post-Nicene Fathers, first series, volume nine (Edinburgh, 1890)

Church of the Triune God (The), The Cyprus Agreed Statement of the International Commission for Anglican-Orthodox Theological Dialogue (London, 2006)

Clement of Rome, *First Letter to the Corinthians*, translated in *Early Christian Writings* by Staniforth, Maxwell (London, 1968)

Condren, Charles de, *The Eternal Sacrifice*, translated by Monteith A J (London, 1906)

Constitutions and Canons Ecclesiastical 1604, with notes by L V Bullard (London, 1934)

Cyprian of Carthage, *Ad Donatum*, translated and edited by Molager, Jean (Paris, 1982)

De la Taille, Maurice, *Mysterium Fidei, de augustissimo corporis et sanguinis Christi sacrificio et sacramento* (Paris, 1931)

Decrees of the Ecumenical Councils, edited by Tanner, Norman & Alberigo, Guiseppe (two volumes, London, Washington, 1990)

Dictionnaire de Théologie Catholique (Paris, 1903–50)

Dix, Gregory, *The Shape of the Liturgy* (London, 1943, 2005)

Dupuy, Michel, *Bérulle et le Sacerdoce* (Paris, 1969)

Durandus of Mende, *The Rationale Divinorum of William Durand of Mende. A New Translation of the Prologue and Book One*, translated by Thibodeau, Timothy (New York, 2007)

Eusebius of Caesarea, *The History of the Church*, translated by Williamson, G A (London, 1965)

Fielding, Henry, *Tom Jones* (Oxford, 1996)

Fincham, Kenneth & Tyacke, Nicholas, *Altars Restored. The Changing Face of English Religious Worship, 1547–c.1700* (Oxford, 2007)

Galot, Jean, *The Theology of Priesthood* (San Francisco, 1985)

Gore, Charles, *The Body of Christ* (London, 1901)

Gregory the Great, *Dialogues*, translated by Zimmermann, Odo (Washington, 1959, 1977)

Gregory the Great, *Forty Gospel Homilies*, translated by Hurst, David (Kalamazoo, 1990)

Gregory of Nazianzus, *Letters*, Library of Nicene and Post-Nicene Fathers, second series, volume seven (Edinburgh, 1893)

Gregory of Nyssa, *Homily on the Baptism of Christ*, Library of Nicene and Post-Nicene Fathers, second series, volume five (Edinburgh, 1892)

Häring, Bernard, *The Law of Christ. Moral Theology for Priests and Laity* (three volumes, Cork, 1963–7)

Häring, Bernard, *This Time of Salvation* (New York, 1966)

Hooker, Richard, *Ecclesiastical Polity* (London 1907, 1925)

Hemming, Laurence, *Worship as a Revelation. The Past, Present and Future of Catholic Liturgy* (London, 2008)

Ignatius of Antioch, *Letter to the Smyrnaeans*, translated in *Early Christian Writings* by Staniforth, Maxwell (London, 1968)

Innocent I, *Church and Worship in Fifth-century Rome: The Letter of Innocent I to Ducentius of Gubbio*, translated and edited by Connell, Martin (Cambridge 2002)

Journet, Charles, *The Mass: the Presence of the Sacrifice of the Cross* (South Bend, 2008)

Justin Martyr, *The Dialogue with Trypho*, translated by Williams, A L (London, 1931)

Lang, Uwe, *Turning Towards the Lord: Orientation in Liturgical Prayer* (San Francisco, 2004)

Lash, Nicholas, *Theology for Pilgrims* (London, 2008)

Leeming, Bernard, *Principles of Sacramental Theology* (second edition, London, 1960)

Leo the Great, *Sermons*, translated by Dolle, Réné (Paris, 2004–)

Lombard, Peter, *Sententiae in IV libris distinctae* (Grottaferrata, 1971–81)

Lubac de, Henri, *Corpus Mysticum. The Eucharist and the Church in the Middle Ages*, edited by Hemming, Laurence & Parsons, Susan (London, 2006)

More, Paul, & Cross, F Leslie, *Anglicanism. The Thought and Practice of the Church of England, Illustrated from the Religious Literature of the Seventeenth Century* (London, 1935)

Newman, John Henry, *An Essay on the Development of Christian Doctrine* (Notre Dame, 1989)

Nichols, Aidan, *Looking at the Liturgy. A Critical View of its Contemporary Form* (San Francisco, 1996)

Nockles, Peter, *The Oxford Movement in Context. Anglican High Churchmanship 1760–1857* (Cambridge, 1994)

O'Collins, Gerald & Jones, Michael Keenan, *Jesus Our Priest. A Christian Approach to the Priesthood of Christ* (Oxford, 2010)

Olier Jean-Jacques, *L'Esprit des cérémonies de la messe: explication des cérémonies de la grand'messe de paroisse selon l'usage romaine* (Perpignon, 2004)

Origen, *Prayer: An Exhortation to Martyrdom*, translated by O'Meara, John (London, 1953)

Pickstock, Catherine, *After Writing. On the Liturgical Consummation of Philosophy* (Oxford, 1998)

Pieper, Joseph, *The Four Cardinal Virtues* (Notre Dame, 1966)

Pius XII, Encyclical Letter *Mediator Dei* (Rome, 1947)

Ratzinger, Joseph, *God and the World. Believing and Living in Our Time. A Conversation with Peter Seewald* (San Francisco, 2002)

Ratzinger, Joseph, *The Spirit of the Liturgy* (San Francisco, 2000)

Salmanticenses, *Cursus Theologiae Moralis* (six volumes, Venice, 1750)

Saward, John, *Cradle of Redeeming Love. The Theology of the Christmas Mystery* (San Francisco, 2002)

Stone, Darwell, *A History of the Doctrine of the Holy Eucharist* (two volumes, Eugene, 2006)

Taylor, Jeremy, *The Great Exemplar of Sanctity and Holy Life According to the Christian Institution in the History of the Life and Death of the Ever Blessed Jesus Christ the Saviour of the World* (London, 1649)

Taylor, Jeremy, *The Rule and Exercises of Holy Living* (Oxford, 1989)

Teresa of Avila, *The Book of Her Life*, in The *Collected Works of St. Teresa of Avila* translated by Kavanaugh, Kieran & Rodriguez, Otilio (volume one, Washington, 1987)

Vonier, Anscar, *A Key to the Doctrine of the Eucharist* (Bethesda, 2003)

Ware, Kallistos, *The Orthodox Church* (London, 1983)

Yannaras, Christos, *The Freedom of Morality* (New York, 1984)

Zizioulas, John, *Being as Communion* (London, 1985, 2004)

Index

Abelard, Peter 129
Abraham 70, 77
absolution 7, 119, 122–5, 129,
    130–8, 148, 149
Alexander of Hales *see* Hales,
    Alexander
Amphilochius 83
Andrewes, Lancelot 63, 65
Anglican
    Catechism 34
    formularies 114, 132
Apocalypse 98, 147
Aquinas *see* S. Thomas
Aristotle 8, 19
Arminian reaction 13
Ascension 23
atonement 54–6, 71, 76–9, 81,
    119, 124
Azazel, fallen angel 55

Balthasar, Hans Urs von 110
Baptism 5, 8, 12, 16, 25, 31–2,
    34, 36, 40–1, 47, 65, 86,
    88–9, 120, 122–3, 132,
    134, 136
Barker, Margaret 32–3, 54–6,
    78
beatitude 3, 6–10, 14, 16–17, 21,
    24–6, 36, 45, 47–9, 71–2,
    89, 92, 98, 105–6, 108,
    112, 114, 135, 138, 142,
    144, 146–7, 150

Benedict XVI, Pope 6, 11, 107,
    113, 151 *see*
    also Ratzinger, Joseph
Berengar of Tours 34
    Eucharistic controversy 102
Berger, David 102, 104
Bérulle, Cardinal Pierre de 35,
    36, 93–4
Book of Common Prayer *see*
    Common Prayer, Book of
bread and wine 34, 36, 59, 65,
    68, 70–1, 77, 79, 93, 104
Butler, Christopher 47

Calvary 53–4, 57, 59, 61, 70–2,
    79, 81, 92–3, 143
Casel, Dom Odo 37, 38
Chalcedon, Council of 127
Charles I, king of England 113
Christian moral life 8, 21, 46,
    48, 71, 83, 134
Church of England 2, 14,
    16–17, 92, 114–15, 132–3,
    142
    partitioning 101
Cicero 11, 84
circumcision 31–2
Clement of Rome *see* S.
    Clement
Colossians, letter to 75
Common Prayer, Book of 33,
    64, 114, 131, 148

Condren, Charles de 60
confession 7, 122, 129–33, 135,
   136, 137, 148
Confirmation 34
Corinthians 30, 78, 120
Cosin, John 131
Counter-Reformation 46, 53,
   66, 133
Cranmer, Archbishop 2
Cross (The) 16, 33, 38, 53–4,
   56–7, 60–1, 64, 67–8,
   70–1, 77, 79, 81, 109, 112,
   124, 143, 145
cult
   Christian 3–4, 6, 9, 11, 16,
      22, 37, 49, 97, 111, 113,
      150
   pagan mystery 31
   Solomonic 48
   temple 16, 54, 100
cure of souls 6, 127, 129, 136
Cyprus Agreed Statement 2006
   90–2
Cyril of Jerusalem 83

Day
   of Atonement 55, 56
   of Resurrection 22, 24
Dialogue of Justin *see* S. Justin
   Martyr
Dix, Gregory 67
Docetists 30
Durandus of Mende 102, 104,
   111

Ephesians, letter to 30, 75
Epiphany 23
Eucharist (rite) 34

Fielding, Henry 119
Florence, Council of 32
forgiveness of sin/s 5–7, 67,69,
   119–22, 132–5, 137, 147

Galot, Jean 87
Gore, Charles 60, 79
Guardini, Romano 107

Hales, Alexander of 85
Häring, Bernard 2–3, 17–20, 45
Hebrews, letter to 32, 55–6,
   75–8, 120
Hemming, Lawrence 9, 14,
   24–5, 27, 37–8, 100, 106
Herbert, George 12
Holy
   of Holies 55, 78
   Order 34, 84, 87
   Spirit 20, 24, 43, 45, 65, 82,
      119, 121, 138, 150
Hooker, Richard 1, 3, 5–6,
   14–17, 20, 23, 40–2, 63,
   90, 92, 100–2, 113, 141
Hugh of St Victor 35, 79
Huysmans, Joris Karl 110

Ignatius of Antioch *see* S.
   Ignatius
incarnation 20, 35–6, 38, 42,
   48, 57, 62, 77–8, 80–1, 94,
   106, 143, 147
Inge, Dean William 21

James I, king of England 113
Jerusalem Temple 10, 13, 54,
   100
Jewel, John, bishop 42

justice 3, 6, 8, 11–12, 15, 19, 26, 32, 56, 134–5, 142
Justin Martyr *see* S. Justin Martyr

Kurios Christos 37

Lamb (of God) 80, 82
Last Supper 61–2, 71, 78–9, 81, 94, 99
Latin Church 1, 66, 89, 104, 122, 130, 146
Laudian Movement 15, 63
Liturgical Movement 2, 21, 107–8, 110, 115, 148
Lombard, Peter 34
Lord's Supper 143
Lubac, Henri de 68, 106, 108
Luther, Martin 122
Lutheran
Churches, Scandinavia 142
view 42

marriage 34, 127
martyrdom 7, 24, 126–7, 149
Mass 5, 35, 44, 59, 61, 69, 78, 86, 97, 103, 105, 107, 111, 125
Mosaic
Law 31–2, 48
sacrifices 33
Mozarabic rite 36

Nazareth 55
New
Covenant 31–2, 38, 77, 93, 104
Testament 30–1, 53, 75, 83–4, 88, 93, 97, 120

Newman, Cardinal John Henry 36
Nichols, Aidan 105, 111, 113

Old Testament 37, 54
ordination 5, 83–4, 87–2, 94, 136, 145–6
Origen of Alexandria 12
original sin 31–2
Otto, Rudolph 18
Oxford Movement 113–15, 130, 132, 133

pagan/s 12, 126 *see also* cult and priesthood
rites 31
Parsifal 21–2
Passion 44–5, 57, 59–60, 68, 70, 75, 79, 80–1, 85, 99, 104, 125, 134
Passover 78, 80
Paul VI, Pope 46
penance 34, 86, 122–5, 127–31, 133, 135–7, 148–9
Penitence 7, 134–5, 138, 149
persecution 97, 100, 126–7
Person of Christ 6, 44, 62
Philippians 82
Philo of Alexandria 15
Pickstock, Catherine 21, 70, 102, 105–6
Pilate, Pontius 45
Pius X, Pope 68
Pius XII, Pope 37
priesthood
Jewish 85
medieval concept of 85

Melchizedek 33, 55, 60, 75,
    77–8, 80, 93
ministerial 1, 3–5, 7, 10, 26,
    81, 83, 86–7, 93–4, 119,
    135–6, 145, 149–150
pagan 85
Primary Russian Chronicle 25
Puritan/s 15–16, 23, 113, 149
ideology 100
party 16

Radical Orthodoxy 6, 107
Ratzinger, Joseph 103, 107–10,
    114–15 *see also* Benedict
    XVI
Reformation 26, 58, 66–7, 89,
    110, 115, 145
see also Counter-Reformation
Benedictine 110
English 63, 113
repentance 7, 31, 48, 54, 82, 88,
    119, 120, 122–3, 125, 128,
    133, 135, 138
Roman Canon 35, 67
Romans, letter to 75, 82

S. Alphonsus de Liguori 2, 103,
    130
S. Ambrose 84
S. Augustine of Hippo 6, 9, 12,
    18, 31, 34–5, 42, 53, 56,
    58, 60, 66, 69, 84–5, 88–9,
    91–2, 110, 123, 130, 143,
    146
S. Clement of Rome, Pope 33,
    83
S. Cyprian 31, 33, 66, 83, 88
S. Gregory

the Great, Pope 66, 84–5,
    129, 135
Nazianzus 83–4
of Nyssa 91
S. Ignatius of Antioch 30, 58,
    97
S. John
the Apostle 120
the Baptist 119
Chrysostom 68, 84–5
of Damascus 13
Eudes 37
S. Justin Martyr 58
Dialogue of 89
S. Paul 30, 56, 77–8, 82, 97,
    120
doctrine 125
teaching 32, 43
S. Peter 20, 32, 81, 119, 121
S. Teresa of Avila 24
S. Thomas Aquinas 11–14, 16,
    19, 24, 27, 30–1, 35, 43–4,
    54, 56, 61–2, 64–5, 67,
    70, 75, 78, 85–7, 98–100,
    102–3, 110–11, 119, 122,
    124, 134, 144
S. Zephyrinus, Pope 102
Sabbath 23, 109
Saward, John 36, 37
schism, Donatist 88
Second Coming 45, 49
Second Vatican Council 1, 18,
    37, 46, 102, 107–10, 133,
    137, 144, 146

Tabernacle 10, 26, 45, 49, 101
Taille, Maurice de la 60
Taylor, Jeremy 63–6, 93

Temple 10, 13, 16, 26, 32–3, 55,
    60, 71, 75–6, 78, 80, 82–3,
    93, 97, 100, 150
  of Jerusalem 10, 54, 100
  Jewish 101
  Solomonic 16
Tertullian 33, 66, 83, 88
transubstantiation 42, 63–4
Trent, Council of 25, 32, 34,
    42, 61, 64, 68–9, 89,
    103–4, 122, 124, 129
Tyre, basilica 98

Unction 86
  of the Sick 34

virtue
  charity 12, 19
  classification of 11
  faith 12, 19, 35
  heroic 24

hope 12, 19
justice 3, 11–12, 19, 26. 56
moral 8, 12, 19
natural 20, 24, 43
sacrificial 41–2
theolological 19, 21, 26, 32,
    38, 43
Visitation of the Sick 131
Vonier, Dom Anscar 5, 44,
    53–4, 56, 59, 61–2, 64,
    103–4

Wagner, Richard 21–2

Yannaras, Christos 2, 7, 9,
    126–9, 136, 149

Zechariah, prophesy 14
Zephyrinus, Pope *see* S.
    Zephyrinus
Zizioulas, John 45, 91, 93